I

THE INFINITE REALITY

Knowing Oneself in a Fast-Paced Distracted World

Jayan Menon

Imprint

Published in India by Notion Press
Printed and distributed in India by Notion Press

Dedication

To my parents who taught me the meaning of integrity and stood by me as I learned when and how to live it. Their example has been my compass - steady, silent, and always true.

This Page has been intentionally left Blank

Note from the Author

For many years, I pursued what the world often calls success. And in many ways, I attained it. But amid the constant demands, decisions, and daily routines, I began to feel a quiet but persistent pull - a sense that something essential was missing. That pull became a question. And that question would not leave me: Who am I, really?

It was not a crisis. It was a turning point. This question led me on a journey - one that traversed ancient and modern philosophies, religion, spirituality, science, and psychological studies. I read deeply. I reflected constantly. And I watched - not just myself, but the people around me: ambitious professionals, thoughtful seekers, overwhelmed parents, and quiet observers. Each, in their own way, was living through the same question.

Depending on our upbringing, environment, or personal priorities, we often come to identify ourselves by what we do, how we look, what we have studied, how we eat or dress, where we live, or the relationships we hold. These are the ways the world sees us. But beneath all that, I began to ask: What am I to myself?

This book is the culmination of that exploration. It brings together insights from Advaita Vedanta, Buddhism, and Stoicism -systems that have stood the test of time in helping us look inward. But it also engages with the empirical lens of modern science and psychology, allowing us to understand how the mind works, how identity forms, and why meaning can sometimes feel elusive - even when everything appears outwardly successful.

What emerged is not a doctrine. Nor is it a conclusion. It is a pause - an invitation to reflect, to realign, and to rediscover that part of yourself that existed before titles, roles, and expectations. Looking back, I often wish that my younger self had known even a few of these insights. The journey might have been much more joyful - even if nothing outside had changed. No matter where you are in life, if you have ever felt the quiet nudge to look inward - this book is for you.

Jayan Menon

Contents

IV. Relationships, Roles, and Desire

V. Meaning, Motivation, and Purpose

VI. The Expanding Self in a Changing World

VII. Unveiling the Real – The Path to Liberation

This Page has been intentionally left Blank

Introduction

The stars do not wonder why they shine. The rivers do not ask where they are going. The trees do not seek applause for growing tall. They simply exist - unfolding in perfect rhythm with the universe, without doubt, without resistance.

And yet, here I am - thinking, analysing, questioning. Why am I different? Why do I, unlike everything else in nature, feel the need to seek meaning, purpose, and identity?

For much of my life, I lived by an idea of who I was supposed to be. That idea was not mine to begin with - it was handed down, shaped by culture, family, society. Before I could even form independent thoughts, I had already absorbed the rules of the world: what is right and wrong, what is worth striving for, what success looks like, and what failure means.

Some of these ideas offered structure and direction. But along with them came something else - expectations, fears, attachments, and limits. Without realizing it, I began to live as a reflection of what others thought I should be.

I came to believe that I am this name, this story, this role, this body. But what if that's only a fragment of the truth? What if the "I" I have been living as is not the whole picture at all? What if the real "I" is not just personal, but profound - far beyond anything I have ever been taught?

Why Ask These Questions?

It is easy to live life without ever questioning. Most of us do. The world keeps us occupied - goals to chase, problems to solve, roles to fulfil. There is always something that demands our attention. So, we go on, distracted, driven; rarely stopping to ask the one question that could change everything:

Who is the one experiencing all this?

That question only surfaces when something cracks our carefully built life. When a loss strips away what we thought we needed. When success arrives but doesn't fulfil. When relationships shift, or identity collapses, and we are left wondering - if all that can change, what remains?

These moments, painful as they are, offer a doorway. They force us to turn inward, to ask what lies beneath all the noise and striving.

What Makes This Book Different?

There are countless books on self-discovery, spirituality, psychology, and philosophy. Some offer ancient wisdom. Others offer modern frameworks. Some are rooted in faith, others in science. This book brings them all together - not to create a new system, but to dissolve the ones we unconsciously live by.

It is not tied to any single belief, religion, or ideology. Instead, it draws from many - Advaita, Buddhism, neuroscience, psychology, real-life experiences - to explore one simple yet powerful question: Who am I, really?

This is not a theoretical exercise. It is an invitation to pause, reflect, and observe - to connect knowledge with personal experience. To ask not just, "Is this idea true?" but "Does this feel true in my own life?"

What You will Find Here

This book is built on four foundations: (i) Science and psychology – how the mind works, how conditioning shapes us, why we seek, and why we suffer. (ii) Philosophical traditions – timeless perspectives on the nature of the self, impermanence, and truth. (iii) Real-life experience – stories, struggles, and insights from my own life and others who have walked this path. (iv) Reflection – not to hand you answers, but to help you see the beliefs you already carry - many of which you may never have questioned.

Each chapter brings these strands together, not to give you a new identity, but to help you see beyond the one you have been given. This is not a book of spiritual promises or quick-fix answers. It is a mirror. A gentle invitation to remember what you already are - and always have been. What you find here may not always be comfortable. But it will be real. And that is where freedom begins.

Who is "I" in this Book?

Before we go further, it's important to clarify something. The "I" in this book is **not the author**. It is not a personal identity or a fixed personality. It is the "I" that exists at the heart of every human experience - the silent witness that thinks, feels, dreams, doubts, and wonders.

When you read the word "I" in these pages, you might feel that I am speaking from my perspective. And that's true. But more deeply, I am speaking from a place we all share.

Because no matter who you are - your name, background, beliefs, successes, or failures - you also refer to yourself as "I." You experience joy. You feel pain. You think thoughts. You carry dreams. You have fears. You seek meaning. And that seeking - that mystery of who you really are beneath all the layers - is what this book is about.

So, this book is not about *me*. It is about *you*. Not in the sense of telling you what your journey should be - but in offering a space to explore about what do *you* believe about yourself, where did those beliefs come from and what happens if you loosen their grip?

The "I" in this book is the same "I" that exists in you. It is not the body, or the mind, or the story. It is the awareness behind them all. Timeless. Wordless. Ever-present. And it is to *that* I that this book is written.

Before any path can be walked, one must ask: who is walking it? As you begin this journey, pause. Let the 'I' you read not be someone else's voice, but your own - the one that wonders, observes, and seeks. This is where your inquiry begins.

Section I

The Basis of the Journey

Exploring the Nature of "I"

Chapter 1

My Evolution

The sense of "I" that each of us experiences today did not emerge in isolation, nor is it merely a product of recent history. It is the outcome of millions of years of evolutionary pressures - shaped, refined, and reinforced long before the first civilizations arose, long before language was invented, even before conscious thought as we know it existed.

Long ago, survival was a moment-to-moment challenge. Our ancestors lived in an environment where food was uncertain, predators were many, and the dangers of injury, disease, or exile could quickly become fatal. In such a world, certain psychological patterns proved advantageous. Over countless generations, the human brain evolved around them - not to seek truth or happiness, but to maximize survival.

This evolutionary inheritance laid the groundwork for many of the traits I recognize within myself even today.

The Instincts Beneath "I"

The early human who was cautious of rustling in the bushes - even if it was just the wind - was more likely to survive than the one who dismissed it. Thus, a bias towards fear, suspicion, and hypervigilance became part of our inheritance. Today, this bias lives on in my anxiety about uncertain futures, my hesitation before new opportunities, my mental rehearsals of "what could go wrong."

In small tribes, survival depended on social bonds. Rejection or exile often meant death. This deep need for acceptance, for approval, for belonging is encoded in my mind. Today, even in vast cities, where I could theoretically live without knowing my neighbours, I feel the sting of social rejection, the need for validation, the pull toward conformity.

Access to resources - food, mates, protection - was often determined by one's standing in the group. Evolution favoured those who competed, who compared, who sought status and recognition. Even now, I find myself measuring my worth through achievements, possessions, accolades - desires deeply rooted not in greed, but in survival.

In a world where tomorrow was uncertain, it made sense to prioritize immediate gains over long-term plans. This wiring persists. Even today, I might choose short-term gratification over long-term benefit, whether through eating habits, financial decisions, or emotional reactions.

Evolution Is Not Destiny

Understanding these inherited tendencies is not about blame or guilt. It is not about judging myself for being fearful, status-driven, impatient, or approval-seeking. It is about recognizing that these tendencies are ancient survival strategies, operating within a mind built for a very different world.

But evolution did not stop with instincts. It also gifted humans a profound ability - to reflect. Unlike most other creatures, I can observe my own thoughts. I can step outside my reactions. I can choose not to be ruled by every impulse. In this capacity for self-awareness lies the possibility of transcending my evolutionary inheritance.

Yes, my mind instinctively recoils from uncertainty - but I can lean into it, knowing growth lies there. It craves validation - but I can anchor my worth internally, not externally. It seeks immediate comfort - but I can choose patience, discipline, and long-term fulfilment.

Evolution Continues Within Me

If I were merely a bundle of inherited instincts, my path would be predetermined. But the arc of human history tells a different story. Time and again, individuals and societies have challenged their basic instincts - to cooperate instead of compete, to include instead of exclude, to sacrifice comfort for a greater ideal.

Every act of kindness, creativity, courage, and compassion is an act of transcending pure survival programming. Within my own life, every moment of mindfulness, every decision to choose growth over fear, every instance where I resist the easy path in favour of the meaningful one, is a quiet revolution against blind inheritance.

Evolution is not over. It continues - within each choice I make, within each awareness I cultivate.

A Foundation for the Journey Ahead

As I move toward exploring the scientific, psychological, and philosophical views of "I," it is important to remember: The "I" that questions, seeks, suffers, and aspires is built on the vast scaffolding of evolution. My instincts are ancient, but my awareness is timeless.

Evolution brought me this far. Awareness invites me to go further. I am not only a product of my past. I am the possibility of my own future.

While evolution explains the ancient forces that shaped the tendencies within me, it is modern science that peels back the layers even further. What once was survival instinct has now become neural networks, chemical signals, and dynamic brain processes - quietly shaping every thought, every feeling, every idea of 'I.'

To understand myself more deeply, I must now step into the scientific lens - to see how biology, chemistry, and the architecture of the brain continue to weave the intricate story of who I believe myself to be.

Chapter 2

The Scientific View of "I"

For centuries, philosophers have debated the nature of selfhood, but only in recent decades has science provided concrete insights into what we call "I." Neuroscientists, cognitive scientists, and behavioural researchers have uncovered fascinating truths about how the brain constructs identity, how motivations shape us, and how relationships influence our perception of self. But does science offer a complete picture of who we are? Or does it merely explain the mechanics behind our experience while leaving deeper existential questions unanswered?

Modern neuroscience and psychology challenge and redefine our understanding of identity, motivation, and selfhood. It questions whether we are truly in control of our thoughts and desires or if we are merely the result of neural processes and biological conditioning.

The Brain and the Self: Constructing "I"

At first glance, it seems that "I" is an obvious and unchanging entity. We wake up every day with a sense of being the same person we were yesterday. But what creates this continuity? According to neuroscience, the self is not a fixed thing - it is an ongoing process.

Different regions of the brain contribute to our experience of selfhood. The prefrontal cortex is responsible for decision-making, personality, and social behaviour, playing a key role in how we construct our identity. The default mode network (DMN), a collection of interconnected brain regions, activates when we are not engaged in tasks, creating the constant mental chatter that reinforces our sense of self. Meanwhile, the hippocampus stores memories, ensuring that we remember past experiences that define who we think we are.

Yet, despite these systems working in unison, neuroscientists have discovered that there is no single "self-centre" in the brain. Instead, identity arises from multiple processes working together. This suggests that the "I" we take for granted is more of a story our brain tells us rather than an independently existing entity.

The Illusion of Selfhood: Neuroscience and Identity

One of the most groundbreaking discoveries in neuroscience comes from split-brain studies conducted by Roger Sperry and Michael Gazzaniga. In patients whose brain hemispheres were surgically separated to treat epilepsy, scientists found that each hemisphere formed its own version of "I."

In one experiment, when the left hemisphere of a split-brain patient was shown an image and asked to explain it, the right hemisphere - which did not see the image - would create a completely different story to make sense of it. This revealed that selfhood is not unified but rather a construct emerging from fragmented brain processes.

Further studies have shown that damage to certain brain areas can completely alter personality, memory, or sense of self. If selfhood is just the result of brain activity, then who are we when our brain changes? This raises a fundamental question - if my "I" can change based on brain function, what truly remains constant?

Dopamine and Motivation: Why We Keep Chasing More

Throughout human history, people have believed that achieving wealth, power, or external success would bring lasting happiness. But scientific studies show that the brain is wired for constant seeking, not contentment.

Research by Dr. Robert Sapolsky at Stanford University reveals that dopamine, the "reward chemical," is not actually about pleasure - it is about anticipation. This means that we derive more excitement from chasing something than from attaining it. The moment we achieve something, the brain resets and looks for the next thing to pursue.

This explains why people experience fleeting happiness when they get a promotion but soon desire another, buy a new car or house but quickly grow accustomed to it or achieve social recognition but soon seek the next level of validation.

If dopamine keeps us in an endless cycle of wanting more, it forces us to ask: Am I really in control of my desires, or is my brain programming me to always seek?

The Science of Connection: How Relationships Shape Identity

We often think of identity as something purely individual, but research shows that our sense of self is deeply influenced by our social connections.

The Harvard Study of Adult Development, an 80+ year-long study, found that the strongest predictor of long-term happiness and well-being is not wealth, success, or fame - it is strong relationships. People with deep friendships and meaningful family bonds live longer, are healthier, and report greater life satisfaction.

Further research by Dr. Ruth Feldman at Stanford University shows that when people form deep emotional connections their heart rates and breathing patterns synchronize, their brain waves align in rhythm and their hormone levels change in response to each other's presence.

This suggests that our sense of "I" is not isolated but rather interwoven with the people around us. If identity is shaped by relationships, then who am I when I am alone?

Mindfulness and Neuroplasticity: Rewiring the Self

Scientific studies show that the brain is not fixed - it is constantly changing based on experiences, thoughts, and habits. This concept, known as neuroplasticity, reveals that we can reshape our perception of self over time.

Research by Dr. Richard Davidson at the University of Wisconsin demonstrates that mindfulness and meditation rewire the brain, reducing stress and increasing emotional resilience. Functional MRI (fMRI) scans show that long-term meditators have greater grey matter density in areas related to emotional regulation and self-awareness.

Similarly, studies on cognitive behavioural therapy (CBT) show that changing thought patterns can literally alter neural pathways. This means that the "I" we believe ourselves to be is not permanent - it is flexible, evolving, and shaped by our attention and habits.

Conclusion: What Does Science Say About "I"?

Modern science challenges traditional notions of identity and reveals several key insights: The self is not a single, fixed entity - it is a collection of brain processes. The brain constructs identity as an ongoing narrative, not an absolute truth. Dopamine keeps us in a loop of seeking, rather than finding lasting contentment. Relationships and social interactions deeply shape our sense of self. Mindfulness and neuroplasticity show that identity is not fixed - it can be reshaped.

These findings force us to rethink who we are and whether our sense of self is as real as we believe. If identity is constantly shifting, then what truly remains unchanged?

Some questions remain unanswered

Science provides a framework for understanding "how" the brain constructs identity, but it does not answer deeper questions such as: Is there a self beyond the brain? If identity is flexible, does that mean "I" am just an illusion? How do I find meaning if everything is constantly changing?

The subjective experience of identity, meaning, and self-awareness is perhaps best understood through the lens of psychology and philosophy.

Chapter 3

The Psychological View of "I"

Science tells us that the brain constructs identity, but psychology takes the discussion further - how do I experience myself? My thoughts, emotions, relationships, and experiences all shape my understanding of who I am. But are these entirely my own, or have they been conditioned by my upbringing and environment?

From childhood, I was taught certain values, fears, and expectations. These shaped the way I see myself, what I believe I am capable of, and what I think I deserve. But as I have grown, I have begun to question: What if my identity is not entirely my own? What if it is shaped by forces, I was never aware of?

Psychology influences our sense of self, from early childhood attachments to the stories we tell ourselves about success, failure, and purpose.

Attachment and Self-Perception: How Early Bonds Define Us

Psychologists John Bowlby and Mary Ainsworth introduced Attachment Theory, which explains how the bonds we form in early childhood influence the way we relate to others - and ourselves - throughout life. They classified it as Secure attachment (formed when a child receives consistent care and emotional support) which leads to confidence and resilience and Insecure attachment (formed when a child experiences neglect, unpredictability, or emotional detachment) which can lead to anxiety, low self-esteem, or fear of abandonment.

These early patterns do not just shape how we form relationships - they shape how we see ourselves. If I was made to feel loved and valued as a child, I grow up believing that I am worthy. If I felt abandoned or unimportant, I may struggle with self-doubt and a constant need for validation.

But psychology also tells us that we are not trapped by our early experiences. With self-awareness and effort, we can rewire our emotional responses, develop healthier self-esteem, and break free from limiting beliefs imposed on us in childhood.

Maslow's Hierarchy of Needs: The Evolution of Identity

Psychologist Abraham Maslow proposed that human motivation follows a hierarchy, progressing from basic survival needs to higher levels of self-actualization. These are (i) Physiological Needs: Food, water, shelter - the foundation of existence, (ii) Safety Needs: Security, financial stability, freedom from fear, (iii) Belongingness Needs: Relationships, family, friendships, and social identity (iv) Esteem Needs: Achievement, recognition, self-respect and (v) Self-Actualization: Finding meaning, fulfilling one's potential.

Where I stand on this hierarchy influences how I define myself. If I am struggling with basic needs, my identity may revolve around survival. If I have achieved security, I may seek purpose and fulfilment.

But the danger is that many people get stuck at a level that is not truly their own. Society often pressures us to seek wealth, recognition, or external success - even if what we really seek is meaning and peace. Understanding Maslow's hierarchy allows me to ask: Am I pursuing what truly matters to me, or just following a script I was given?

Growth vs. Fixed Mindset: How Beliefs Shape Reality

Dr. Carol Dweck's research at Stanford University introduced the concept of growth mindset vs. fixed mindset, which explains why some people overcome challenges while others remain stuck.

A fixed mindset believes that intelligence, talent, and ability are static - "I am either good at something or I am not." A growth mindset believes that effort and learning lead to improvement - "I can get better at anything if I try."

Studies show that people with a growth mindset achieve more, handle setbacks better, and experience greater personal fulfilment. Those with a fixed mindset often avoid challenges, fearing failure.

For much of my life, I unknowingly absorbed a fixed mindset. I believed I was "bad" at certain things, not realizing that ability is fluid. But once I embraced a growth mindset, I saw challenges differently - not as threats to my identity, but as opportunities to expand who I am.

Cognitive Behavioural Therapy: How Thoughts Define the Self

One of the most influential psychological frameworks in modern therapy is Cognitive Behavioural Therapy (CBT), developed by Dr. Aaron Beck and Albert Ellis. CBT demonstrates that our thoughts shape our emotions and actions.

For example: If I believe "I am not good enough," I may avoid opportunities, reinforcing my belief. If I believe "I always fail," I may not try at all, ensuring failure. If I believe "I can learn from mistakes," I will persist, increasing my chances of success.

CBT teaches that thoughts are not always facts - they are interpretations. By challenging and changing limiting thoughts, we can reshape how we see ourselves.

When I first encountered this idea, I questioned: How many of my fears and limitations are real, and how many are just stories I have told myself? And if they are just stories, can I rewrite them?

Success, Failure, and the Stories We Tell Ourselves

For most of my life, I was taught that success is something to chase, and failure is something to fear. But psychology tells us that our definitions of success and failure are not universal - they are learned.

Some cultures define success as financial achievement, others as spiritual wisdom. Some families praise academic excellence, others value creative freedom. Some people see failure as shameful; others see it as essential to growth.

The work of Dr. Martin Seligman, a pioneer in positive psychology, shows that the way we interpret setbacks determines our well-being. People who view failure as temporary and solvable tend to be resilient. Those who see failure as personal and permanent tend to give up easily.

When I redefined success on my own terms, I no longer felt trapped by external expectations. I realized that the true failure was not trying, not learning, and not evolving.

Conclusion: What Does Psychology Say About "I"?

Psychology challenges the idea that "I" is an independent, unchanging entity. Instead, it reveals that: Our earliest attachments shape how we see ourselves. Our motivations are influenced by external conditioning, often without our awareness. Our mindset determines whether we see ourselves as limited or capable of growth. Our thoughts shape our emotions and reality - but thoughts can be changed. Success and failure are not absolute - they are narratives that we can redefine.

If my sense of self is shaped by childhood, by society, by unconscious beliefs - then who am I beneath all these influences?

Some Questions that remain Unanswered

Psychology provides insight into why I feel the way I do about myself, but it does not fully explain the deeper question: Who am I beyond my thoughts, beyond conditioning, beyond personal history?

If psychology tells me that identity is constructed, then what remains when I strip away everything that was given to me? We turn to philosophy to answer the questions: Is there an "I" beyond the mind? Is identity just an illusion? What is real and what is merely perception?

Chapter 4

The Philosophical View of "I"

*"Science is what you know. Philosophy is what you don't know." -
Bertrand Russell*

Science gives us a framework for understanding how the self is constructed, and psychology explains why we think and behave the way we do. But neither fully answers the deeper existential question - who am I beyond my thoughts, beyond my body, beyond everything I have been conditioned to believe?

This is where philosophy steps in. Throughout history, different philosophical traditions have explored the nature of self, identity, and reality. Some argue that the self is an illusion, a fleeting construct of mind and body. Others suggest that beneath the changing experiences of life, there exists something permanent - a deeper, infinite self.

I explored four major philosophical perspectives - Advaita Vedanta, Stoicism, Existentialism, and Buddhism. Each offers a unique way to understand the self, suffering, and liberation.

Advaita Vedanta: The Infinite Self Beyond Identity

One of the most profound perspectives on the self comes from Advaita Vedanta, a school of Hindu philosophy that asserts that the "I" we identify with is not our true self. According to Advaita, our real nature is not the body, not the mind, not the changing personality - but something far greater: pure awareness, infinite and eternal.

The fundamental teaching of Advaita is "*Aham Brahmasmi*" - "I am Brahman." This means that my essence is not separate from the universe - it is the universe. The same consciousness that animates the stars, the trees, and all living beings is the same "I" that experiences life through this body and mind.

But why, then, do I feel separate? Why do I suffer? According to Advaita, this is because of Maya, the illusion of separateness. From birth, I am conditioned to believe that I am just this body, just this name, just this identity. I forget my deeper nature and become trapped in the cycle of attachment, fear, and suffering.

The way to break free, according to Advaita, is through self-inquiry - asking "Who am I?" beyond all labels and roles. The moment I realize that I am not the temporary self but the eternal awareness behind it, suffering begins to dissolve.

Stoicism: Mastering Perception and Inner Strength

While Advaita Vedanta focuses on the eternal self, Stoicism, an ancient Greek philosophy, takes a practical approach to the self and suffering. According to Stoicism, the greatest cause of suffering is not what happens to us, but how we interpret it.

The Stoic philosopher Epictetus famously said, *"It is not events that disturb us, but our interpretation of them."*

This means that external events - failure, loss, success, pain - are neutral. It is only my perception that makes them good or bad. If I lose my job, I may see it as a disaster, or I may see it as an opportunity. If someone insults me, I may feel offended, or I may see it as meaningless.

The Stoics taught that true freedom comes not from controlling the world, but from controlling my response to it. If I train myself to see things objectively, I will suffer far less.

This philosophy offers a powerful tool: if I cannot change something, I can at least change how I see it. This aligns with modern psychology, particularly Cognitive Behavioural Therapy (CBT), which teaches that by changing thought patterns, we can change our emotional state.

Existentialism: Creating Meaning in an Uncertain World

While Advaita Vedanta suggests that identity is an illusion, and Stoicism teaches detachment from suffering, Existentialism takes a different approach.

Philosophers like Jean-Paul Sartre and Viktor Frankl argue that life has no inherent meaning. There is no predefined purpose, no universal truth about "who I am." Instead, I must create my own meaning.

Viktor Frankl, a Holocaust survivor and psychiatrist, developed a philosophy called Logotherapy based on his experience in Nazi concentration camps. He found that the prisoners who survived were not necessarily the strongest, but the ones who had a reason to live - a purpose, something greater than themselves. His conclusion was simple: A person who has a "why" can endure any "how."

Existentialism challenges me to ask: What gives my life meaning? Am I living based on my own values, or just following what society expects? If life is uncertain, what do I choose to stand for? Rather than waiting for some external force to define me, Existentialism asks me to take responsibility for creating my own identity and purpose.

Buddhism: The Impermanence of All Things

Whereas Advaita Vedanta speaks of an eternal self and Stoicism focuses on emotional resilience, Buddhism teaches that all suffering comes from attachment - to identity, success, relationships, and even life itself.

According to Buddhist philosophy, everything in life is impermanent - our body, our thoughts, our experiences. But we suffer because we resist change. We want things to remain stable, but they never do.

The Four Noble Truths of Buddhism describe the nature of suffering: These noble truths being (i) Life is suffering (Dukkha) - because everything changes. (ii) Suffering comes from attachment - we cling to things that are temporary. (iii) Letting go ends suffering - when we stop attaching, we stop suffering. (iv) The Eightfold Path - a way to live with wisdom and inner peace.

Buddhism challenges me to ask: What am I holding onto that causes me suffering? Do I resist change because I fear losing my identity? If everything is temporary, can I learn to embrace uncertainty instead of fearing it?

Philosophy, across cultures and time, has explored questions of existence, identity, and meaning. Different traditions have provided unique ways of understanding life - some focusing on ethics, others on society, and some on the material world. A natural question arises: Why focus on only these four - Advaita Vedanta, Stoicism, Existentialism, and Buddhism - when many others exist?

The answer lies in the nature of the inquiry. If the question were about how to build a just society, Confucianism or political philosophy might be central. If the question were about logic and language, analytic philosophy might take precedence. But this book revolves around the most fundamental question: Who am I?

This is not just a theoretical inquiry - it is an attempt to understand the nature of the "I" that experiences everything, the self that seeks, suffers, hopes, and ultimately wonders if it is more than its circumstances.

Not all philosophies are directly concerned with this question, but these four stand out because they each offer a unique yet deeply relevant approach to it.

Each of these four perspectives directly engages with the nature of "I" - whether by questioning its existence, redefining its agency, strengthening its resilience, or showing a path to freedom from suffering.

Other philosophies, while valuable, do not focus as directly on the nature of self. Some deal primarily with ethics, politics, or logic, while others emphasize external societal structures. The relevance of any philosophy depends on the questions being asked, and these four are chosen because they are the most directly relevant to understanding the self, perception, meaning, and freedom.

That said, no philosophy holds absolute answers. The intent is not to exclude but to explore, and this exploration does not end with these four - it begins here.

Conclusion: What Does Philosophy say about "I"?

Philosophy provides multiple perspectives on identity and suffering. Each tradition offers a different answer: Advaita Vedanta says I am not my body or mind - I am pure awareness. Stoicism says I cannot control what happens, but I can control how I perceive it. Existentialism says there is no inherent meaning - I must create my own. Buddhism says suffering comes from attachment - I can let go and find peace.

Each of these ideas offers a tool for self-inquiry, but they also lead to a deeper question - if identity is so fluid, what remains constant?

In Summary

Philosophy helps me understand that "I" is not as solid as I once believed. But knowing this is not enough. How do I apply these ideas in real life? If my thoughts shape my experience, how can I change my thinking? If suffering comes from attachment, how do I let go without feeling lost? If meaning is something I create, how do I define success, failure, and purpose on my own terms?

The ensuing chapters, shift from theory to personal experience - exploring how identity is shaped by conditioning, expectations, and unconscious beliefs. If I was not born with a fixed identity, then who or what has shaped the "I" I believe I am today?

This Page has been intentionally left Blank

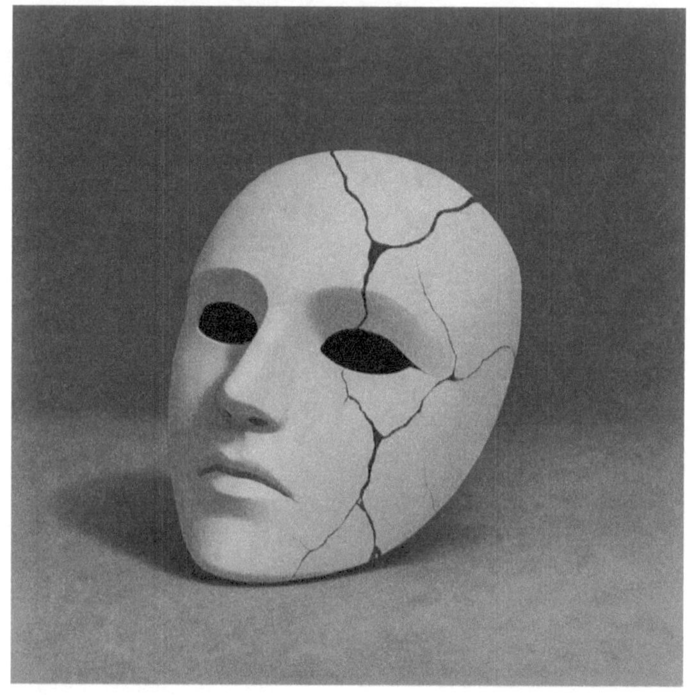

What makes you 'you'? Is it your name, your choices, your memories? Or is there something deeper beneath the surface of your identity? As you move forward, listen not just to what is written, but to what is stirred within you.

Section II

Foundations of the Self

Understanding "I"

Chapter 5

Who Am I?

For as long as I can remember, I have carried a name, an identity, and a history. I have played many roles - child, student, friend, professional, partner, parent. Some of these roles were given to me by birth, while others I sought for myself. I lived within the boundaries of these roles, believing they defined me. But if I strip away these layers, what remains? Who am I, really?

For most of my life, I never questioned this. It seemed obvious. I am a person with a body, a mind, thoughts, feelings, and memories. I am my experiences, my relationships, my achievements, and my failures. Yet, there were moments when this certainty wavered. When I lost something, I thought defined me - my job, a relationship, an ambition - I still existed. When I changed my opinions, beliefs, or values, I was still "me." Even when I could not recognize myself in a past version of who I once was, something remained unchanged. This realization led me to an unsettling question: If everything about me can change, then what is truly 'me'?

Am I My Body?

At first, I thought: I am this body. It made sense. My body is what others see. It is what carries me through life, what enables me to experience pleasure and pain, health and illness, strength and weakness. My physical presence is undeniable; it is tangible and measurable. But when I reflected on it, I realized that my body has never remained the same. The body I had as a child no longer exists. The cells that made me years ago have all been replaced. My face, my hands, my posture - all of it has changed over time. The body I have today is different from the body I will have in the future.

And yet, despite these changes, I have always referred to myself as "I." If my body is always changing, can it really be who I am? If I lose a limb, do I become less "me"? If I grow older and my body weakens, do I become someone else? The deeper I reflected, the clearer it became I have a body, but I am not just my body.

Am I My Mind?

Then I thought: Maybe I am my mind - my thoughts, emotions, and memories. My mind seemed more personal, more intrinsic to who I was. It is my mind that makes decisions, forms opinions, and remembers who I was yesterday. It is my thoughts that create my experiences, and my emotions that make me feel alive. My personality, my likes and dislikes, my aspirations - all of these seemed to be rooted in my mind.

But when I looked closer, I saw that my thoughts and emotions are constantly shifting. I once believed things I no longer believe today. I have felt happiness one moment and sadness the next, without knowing why. There are days when my mind feels clear and sharp, and others when it feels foggy and confused. If my thoughts and emotions change so easily, can they truly define me? And what about sleep?

Every night, when I fall asleep, my thoughts disappear. My emotions fade. My identity is momentarily forgotten. Yet, when I wake up, I am still "me." If I can exist even when my thoughts are absent, then am I really my mind? The more I questioned it, the more I saw that I have a mind, but I am not just my thoughts.

Am I My Name, My Story, My Roles?

For much of my life, I have been known by a name. People recognize me by it. My name carries a history, a set of experiences, relationships, and responsibilities. But my name was given to me. I did not choose it. And more importantly, it is just a label. If I were called something else, would I be someone else?

My identity has been shaped by my upbringing, my environment, and my circumstances. But people born in the same family, with similar experiences, can turn out to be entirely different individuals. Why is it that siblings, raised under the same roof, often have completely different personalities and worldviews? If identity were simply a product of external influences, then why do people with similar lives evolve in such different ways? If I am not my body, not my mind, not my name, and not my past, then who am I?

The One Who Observes Everything

The more I searched, the more I realized: I am not any one thing. I am the one who observes my body, my thoughts, my emotions, and my experiences. There is something within me that is aware of everything that happens yet remains untouched by it. When I feel happiness, there is something in me that knows, "I am happy." When I feel sadness, there is something in me that knows, "I am sad." Even when I am confused, there is something in me that knows, "I am confused."

This awareness has never changed. From childhood to now, through every experience, through every change, that presence has remained the same. The observer within me has witnessed everything - joys, struggles, growth, and losses - but has itself remained unaltered. If everything in my life can shift, yet something within me remains constant, then could that be the real "I"?

What Does This Mean for My Life?

Understanding this has changed the way I see myself. I still have a body, but I am not just my body. I still have a mind, but I am not just my thoughts. I still have a story, but I am not limited to my past. This realization has given me a new kind of freedom.

If my body changes, I am still me. If my mind shifts, I am still me. If my circumstances rise or fall, I am still me. Nothing external can define or limit what I truly am. The pressures I once felt - the need to prove myself, the fear of change, the attachment to identity - began to loosen their grip. If I am not defined by any one thing, then I do not need to cling so desperately to any of it.

And if that is true, then maybe the greatest question in life is not "Who am I?" but rather "What is stopping me from fully being who I am?"

Chapter 6

What Shapes My Identity?

For most of my life, I have believed that I am an independent individual, shaping my own destiny, making my own choices, and defining who I am. I have taken pride in my decisions, in the things I have accomplished, and in the way I have constructed my life. But when I pause to reflect, I see that much of who I think I have been given to me by the world I was born into. I did not choose my name, yet I identify with it. I did not choose the language I speak, yet it shapes how I think. I did not choose my family, my birthplace, or the first values I was taught, yet they influence how I see the world.

So much of my identity has been constructed without my conscious choice. But if I did not create it, can I truly say it is "mine"? This leads me to a deeper question: How much of my identity is shaped by me, and how much has been shaped for me?

The Unnoticed Influence of My Surroundings

As a child, I did not question the world around me. I simply absorbed it. The way my parents spoke, the things they valued, and the beliefs they held - all of these became part of my early understanding of life. If my family valued education, I was encouraged to study hard. If success was measured by wealth, I learned to admire those who had it. If failure was looked down upon, I became afraid of making mistakes. I grew up adopting these ideas as if they were my own.

But were these truly my thoughts? Or were they simply things I had been taught to believe? As I grew older, I encountered new influences - teachers, friends, media, and society. Each of these added another layer to my identity, reinforcing some beliefs and challenging others. Even my emotions were shaped by what I learned. I felt proud when I achieved what others admired. I felt guilt when I acted against what I had been taught was "right." I felt fear when I considered breaking away from expectations. For the longest time, I never questioned whether these reactions were truly my own. But now, I wonder: Who would I be if I had been raised differently?

The Power of Cultural and Social Conditioning

I once believed that my thoughts and decisions were entirely my own. But the more I observe, the more I see how deeply society conditions me. Every society has its rules - both spoken and unspoken. It tells me what is respectable and what is shameful. It tells me what I should pursue and what I should avoid. It tells me how to behave, what to value, and even how to express emotions.

If I conform, I am rewarded. If I deviate, I am questioned, criticized, or even rejected. And so, without realizing it, I adjust myself - sometimes without even knowing why.

But what happens when the values of society change? A hundred years ago, some careers were looked down upon - now they are celebrated. Certain behaviours that were once unacceptable are now considered normal. The definition of success, beauty, and morality is different across cultures and time periods.

If these rules are constantly shifting, can they really define who I am? And if I simply follow what society tells me, am I truly thinking for myself?

How Much of My Identity Is Truly 'Mine'?

This leads to an unsettling thought: If I strip away everything I was taught - what remains? If I had never been told what to value, what would I choose? If I had never been made to fear failure, would I still hesitate to take risks? If I had never been praised for achievement, would I still desire success?

So much of who I think I am is not actually mine. This does not mean that everything I have learned is false. But it means I must ask: Do these beliefs truly belong to me, or have I simply accepted them without question?

If I had been born in a different time, in a different place, to different parents, with different influences, would I still be "me"? If my deepest fears, ambitions, and desires could have been different under different circumstances, then what part of me is truly, unchangeably mine?

Breaking Free: Choosing My Own Identity

If so much of my identity has been given to me, then I have two choices: I can continue living by the identity I have been handed, or I can examine it, question it, and choose who I truly want to be.

This does not mean rejecting everything I have learned. It means asking myself whether the beliefs I hold still serve me. Does this fear still protect me, or is it holding me back? Do I truly want what I am chasing, or am I chasing it because I was told to? By questioning, I begin to take ownership of my identity.

I can still value hard work, but not because I was told to - because I truly believe in its importance. I can still seek success, but not because society says I should - because it aligns with what I want. I can still follow traditions, but not blindly - only if they add meaning to my life.

In this process, I become free - not because I reject everything, but because I start choosing for myself.

What This Means for My Life

I no longer see myself as just a product of my past. Yes, my environment has shaped me. My experiences have influenced me. But I am not trapped by them. If I can question my beliefs, I can change them. If I can recognize my conditioning, I can outgrow it. If I can see where my fears and desires come from, I can decide whether they are worth holding onto.

I am not just who I was told to be. I am who I choose to become.

Chapter 7

The Illusion of Control

I believed that if I planned well enough, worked hard enough, and made the right decisions, I could control my future. I thought that if I did everything correctly, life would unfold exactly as I wanted. If I made the right choices, I would be successful. If I was careful enough, I could avoid pain. If I anticipated every possible challenge, I would never have to face uncertainty.

But life does not follow my plans. Unexpected things happen. People change. Circumstances shift. Even when I do everything "right," things do not always go as expected.

At first, this frustrated me. Then, it terrified me. I did not want to believe that so much of life was out of my hands. I wanted to believe that if I worked hard enough, if I prepared enough, if I controlled enough variables, I could prevent unwanted outcomes. But the more I resisted this truth, the more I suffered.

The Need for Control: Why We Cling to Certainty

I have often wondered why I struggle so much with the unknown. Why does uncertainty feel so unsettling? The answer is simple - control gives me the illusion of security. If I can control my career, I believe I will always have stability. If I can control my relationships, I believe I will never feel lonely. If I can control my health, I believe I can avoid suffering. If I can control what others think of me, I believe I can protect my self-worth.

But is this really true? Have I ever been completely in control of my future? Have I ever been able to stop time from changing things? Have I ever truly known what is coming next? The answer, no matter how much I resist it, is no. No matter how much I plan, prepare, or predict, life unfolds on its own terms.

What Happens When I Try to Control Everything?

When I try to control life, I find myself in a constant state of struggle. I become anxious about the future, fearing that things won't go my way. I obsess over details, believing that perfection will guarantee success. I resist change, trying to hold on to things that are meant to evolve. I become frustrated when others do not behave as I expect them to. Instead of feeling secure, I feel tense, restless, and drained.

The more I try to control life, the more I realize that I am fighting something far bigger than myself. The harder I hold on, the more painful it becomes when things do not go as planned. The tighter my grip, the more fragile I feel.

What Can I Actually Control?

If I cannot control everything, does that mean I should just give up? Should I stop making an effort altogether? The answer is no. It simply means I should redirect my focus to what is truly within my power.

I may not control what happens, but I control how I respond to it. I cannot control the opportunities that come my way, but I can control how prepared I am for them. I cannot control whether someone loves me forever, but I can control how I love while they are here. I cannot control whether I will succeed, but I can control how much effort I put in. I cannot control what others think of me, but I can control how I see myself.

This realization is liberating. It means that I do not need to control everything to be at peace.

Letting Go of the Uncontrollable

Letting go of control does not mean I stop caring. It does not mean I stop making an effort. It simply means I stop resisting life. I still work hard, but I no longer believe that success is guaranteed. I still love, but I no longer fear loss. I still plan, but I no longer cling to the illusion that life will follow my blueprint.

Instead of trying to force life into my expectations, I allow myself to flow with it. I begin to see that I do not need certainty to feel secure, and I do not need control to be at peace.

And in doing so, I find something I never expected - freedom.

What This Means for My Life

I no longer waste energy trying to control things that are beyond me. I no longer live in fear of the unknown. I no longer fight life - I live it. I shift my focus from controlling the future to fully experiencing the present. I do my best, but I let go of the outcome. I prepare for life, but I accept its unpredictability. I take action, but I release the illusion that I am in control.

And in this surrender, I finally feel at peace.

Chapter 8

The Fear of Change and Impermanence

Everything in my life has changed. Some changes happened so gradually that I barely noticed them, while others arrived like a storm, altering my world in an instant. No matter how much I tried to hold on to the way things were, time continued to move forward, indifferent to my desires.

At times, I welcomed change. When it brought me success, happiness, or love, I embraced it. But when it brought loss, uncertainty, or endings, I feared it. There were moments when I wished I could freeze time, capture a moment, and keep it forever. But life does not work that way.

Change is not something that happens occasionally - it is happening every second. The world around me is changing, my body is changing, my thoughts and emotions are changing. Nothing ever truly stays the same. And yet, I have spent much of my life resisting this truth.

Why Do I Fear Change?

I have often wondered why change feels so unsettling, even when I know it is inevitable. Perhaps it is because change threatens my sense of security. When I become comfortable with something - a routine, a relationship, a way of living - I do not want to lose it.

Change forces me to confront the unknown. It disrupts the familiarity I depend on and reminds me that nothing is truly within my control. It makes me face the fact that no matter how much I build, protect, or plan, I cannot stop life from evolving.

Somewhere deep inside, I know that everything I love - people, places, even parts of myself - will change or fade with time. And that realization terrifies me.

The Pain of Holding On

Whenever I have resisted change, I have suffered. When I clung to relationships that had run their course, I felt trapped in something that no longer felt right. When I tried to hold on to a version of myself that I had outgrown, I felt lost and disconnected.

Holding on does not stop things from changing - it only makes the process more painful. I have tried to recreate past happiness, only to find that it does not feel the same. I have wished for certain moments to last forever, only to be disappointed when they passed.

The tighter my grip, the more painful it is when things slip away. And they always do.

Accepting Impermanence: The Only Constant in Life

If change is inevitable, then why do I fight it? Instead of resisting, what if I embraced it? What if, instead of fearing the end of something, I saw it as the beginning of something new?

I have started to see that impermanence is not something to be feared - it is what makes life meaningful. The fact that nothing lasts forever makes every experience, every moment, precious.

If happiness were permanent, would I truly appreciate it? If I could hold on to everything I love forever, would I value it in the same way? It is the fleeting nature of things that makes them beautiful.

The moments that have passed, the people who have come and gone, the phases of life that have ended - they are all part of my journey. I do not need to mourn their passing; I can be grateful that they were ever part of my life.

How Change Has Helped Me Grow

Some of the hardest changes I have faced - the ones I feared the most - turned out to be the ones that shaped me the most. When things fell apart, I discovered new strength within myself. When I lost something, I made space for something new.

Change has challenged me, but it has also given me opportunities I never imagined. It has forced me to adapt, to learn, to grow. If life had remained the same, I would have remained the same. And I do not want to be the same person forever. The truth is, change does not take away from me - it adds to me.

Letting Go and Moving Forward

I am learning to let go - not just of things, but of my resistance to change itself. I no longer see change as something that happens *to* me, but as something that is part of me. I do not need to fight it. I do not need to fear it. I only need to allow it.

This does not mean I do not feel sadness when something ends. It does not mean I do not struggle with uncertainty. But it does mean that I do not let that sadness or fear stop me from living. I do not have to hold on so tightly. I do not have to fear the future. I only have to trust that whatever comes next will shape me in ways I cannot yet understand.

What This Means for My Life

I no longer waste my energy trying to stop change. Instead, I embrace it.

I cherish the people in my life, knowing that every moment with them is a gift. I appreciate where I am today, knowing that it will not last forever. I welcome new experiences, even when they take me out of my comfort zone.

I still make plans, but I no longer believe that they will unfold exactly as I expect. I still love deeply, but I do not hold on out of fear of losing. I still work hard, but I do not attach my worth to the outcome.

And in doing so, I finally find peace - not in resisting change, but in moving with it.

Chapter 9

Life's Lotteries – What Defines Me and What Do I Overcome?

From the moment I was born, certain things were already decided for me. I did not choose my family, my country, my financial situation, or the social conditions I would grow up in. I did not decide whether I would be born into privilege or struggle, into stability or uncertainty. These were the lotteries of life - random circumstances that shaped my early existence without my control.

Some people are born into wealth, while others must fight for survival. Some are blessed with supportive families, while others face hardship from an early age. Some inherit good health, while others battle illness. From education to career opportunities, from relationships to unexpected challenges, life often appears unfair.

For a long time, I believed that these factors determined my fate. I saw people around me succeed because they had advantages I did not. I saw others struggle despite their intelligence and effort. I asked myself: Am I just a product of my circumstances? How much control do I really have over my life? If life is a lottery, how do I win without being given the winning ticket?

But I also began to see the flip side - if life's struggles are not always within my control, then neither are all my successes. If I take full credit for every achievement, I am ignoring the role that luck, circumstances, and the help of others played in my journey. Just as some struggles are unavoidable, some opportunities are given to me through no effort of my own. Acknowledging this does not take away from my hard work - it simply grounds me in humility and protects me from arrogance.

The Unfairness of Life – Acknowledging Reality

One of the hardest lessons to accept is that life is not fair. Some people will have easier lives than others. Some will succeed effortlessly, while others will fight for every inch of progress. The world is not designed to be equal, and pretending otherwise only leads to frustration.

I have seen people who worked tirelessly but never achieved financial success. I have also seen those born into wealth who never had to worry about money. I have met incredibly talented individuals who never got the recognition they deserved, while others with less talent reached the top through luck and connections.

This realization could have made me bitter, but instead, it forced me to ask: If I cannot control where I started, what can I control? Instead of focusing on what I did not get, I started focusing on what I could do with what I had. At the same time, I learned another important lesson - if I succeed, I must not assume it was purely my own doing.

Recognizing the Role of Luck and Privilege in Success

It is easy to believe that I alone am responsible for my success. After all, I worked hard, made sacrifices, and made the right choices. But is that the full picture? What about the opportunities that came my way, not because of effort, but because of chance? What about the mentors, friends, and family who supported me? What about the unseen factors that worked in my favour - being in the right place at the right time, having the right connections, or simply being born into a certain background?

Humility comes from realizing that no one succeeds entirely on their own. No matter how hard I worked, there were forces beyond my control that helped me along the way. Acknowledging this does not make my efforts meaningless - it makes me grateful rather than arrogant.

This awareness helps me in two ways. It keeps me humble in success. If I believe my success is entirely due to my own brilliance, I may look down on others who struggle. But if I acknowledge that I was also helped by luck, I remain grounded. It also prepares me for loss. If I think success is purely my doing, then when things go wrong, I may blame myself entirely. But if I understand that life has both ups and downs, I do not live in fear of loss.

Recognizing the role of luck and external factors does not weaken my accomplishments - it gives me perspective.

Overcoming the Limitations of My Lottery

There are different types of life's lotteries - some visible, some hidden. Some people struggle financially. Others struggle emotionally. Some have good health but no family support. Others have love but battle illness. Each person's challenges are unique, and comparing them is pointless.

What matters is not who has it harder, but how I navigate my own journey. Instead of seeing my challenges as limitations, I can see them as opportunities for growth. When I recognize that some things are beyond my control, I stop wasting energy wishing things were different. Instead, I focus on what I can change, what I can improve, and how I can move forward despite the odds.

This shift in thinking does not erase hardship, but it makes me stronger than my circumstances.

The Dangers of Believing "I Did It All Alone"

Many successful people fall into the trap of believing that their success is entirely their own making. This belief has consequences. It makes me dismissive of others' struggles. If I believe that hard work is all that matters, I may assume that those who struggle are simply not trying hard enough. This can make me indifferent, even cruel.

It makes me arrogant. If I believe I am entirely self-made, I may start believing I am superior to others. It also makes me afraid of failure. If I take full credit for my success, then failure becomes unbearable. I start fearing loss because I believe it will mean I am not as capable as I thought.

But when I acknowledge the role of luck, I become more grateful. I appreciate the opportunities I have had and do not take them for granted. I become more compassionate. I understand that success is not always about effort, and I do not judge others unfairly. I also become less fearful of loss. If success was partly luck, then failure is also partly luck. I do not see setbacks as a reflection of my worth.

The Mindset of Balance: Effort + Awareness

So, what is the right approach? Should I just rely on luck and hope for the best? No. Hard work and effort still matter. But I must balance effort with awareness. I will work hard, but I will not believe that hard work alone guarantees success. I will strive to create opportunities, but I will not assume I control everything. I will take pride in my success, but I will also be grateful for the factors that helped me. I will learn from failure, but I will not take it as a personal curse.

Life is neither fully in my control nor fully random - it is a mix of effort, circumstances, and luck.

What This Means for My Life

I will not waste time complaining about what I was not given. I will not believe that life is entirely unfair or that I am a victim. Instead, I will focus on what I can change, adapt to what I cannot, and move forward with determination.

At the same time, I will not take full credit for everything I achieve. I will acknowledge that luck, privilege, and support played a role. This will keep me humble, grateful, and less fearful of setbacks.

I will live with the awareness that life's lotteries shape me, but they do not define me. And in this balance - between action and acceptance, effort and humility - I will find both strength and peace.

This Page has been intentionally left Blank

This 'I' that you carry lives in a body, wears clothes, earns a living, and belongs to a world of things. But in all this doing, how often do you pause to see how these things shape your sense of self? These next chapters are about the world you inhabit - and how it inhabits you.

Section III

The Physical and Material Self

Chapter 10

Food and Me – More Than Just Survival

Every day, I eat. Sometimes out of hunger, sometimes out of habit, and sometimes just because food is in front of me. It is such a routine part of life that I rarely stop to think about it. Yet, food is one of the most fundamental aspects of survival. Without it, I cannot live.

But food is more than just fuel for my body. It is comfort. It is identity. It is culture. It is emotion.

I have eaten to nourish myself, but I have also eaten to celebrate, to mourn, to distract, and to escape. Food has been a source of both pleasure and guilt. It has been a necessity and a desire, a need and an indulgence.

For something so essential, I have never really questioned its place in my life. What role does food truly play? And how much of my relationship with it is shaped by the world around me rather than by my own needs?

The Evolution of My Relationship with Food

As a child, I ate whatever was given to me. Food was not a choice - it was simply part of my routine. I did not question whether it was healthy or unhealthy, right or wrong. I ate when I was hungry, and I stopped when I was full.

Then, at some point, food became more than just sustenance.

I began to associate certain foods with emotions. A favourite dish became linked to feelings of warmth and love. Special meals were tied to celebrations. Sweets became a reward. Spicy foods became a test of endurance. Some foods were considered prestigious, while others were seen as basic necessities.

I started to see food not just as nourishment but as a reflection of status, culture, and personal choices. The way I ate was no longer just about hunger - it was about identity.

Vegetarianism, Non-Vegetarianism, and Ethical Eating

One of the biggest divides in food choices is between vegetarianism and non-vegetarianism. For some, eating meat is a cultural norm, something passed down for generations. For others, it is a personal choice, guided by ethical, religious, or health reasons. In some traditions, food is considered sacred, and the act of eating is tied to spiritual beliefs.

Many people choose vegetarianism for reasons beyond taste or tradition. Some choose it with the idea that animals should not be harmed unnecessarily. Some believe plant-based diets are healthier and reduce the risk of diseases. Many religions encourage vegetarianism as a way to cultivate non-violence. Some view producing plant-based food has a lower impact on the environment than animal farming.

Hinduism, Jainism, and Buddhism, in different ways, encourage ahimsa (non-violence) in food choices. Jain food, for example, excludes not only meat but also root vegetables like onions and garlic, as pulling them out harms the plant entirely. Some Buddhists follow a vegetarian diet, while others eat meat that has not been killed specifically for them.

For many, food is not just about nutrition but about karma - what we consume affects us beyond just the body.

For others, eating meat is a natural part of life. In colder climates, where plant-based diets are hard to sustain, meat is essential. Many cultures have long histories of hunting, fishing, and animal farming. Some argue that animal protein provides essential nutrients that are harder to obtain from plants alone. Some people reject imposed dietary restrictions, believing that food should be a personal decision.

While vegetarianism emphasizes non-violence, many non-vegetarians argue that nature itself is built on consumption. Animals eat other animals. Even plants, though they seem passive, consume resources and compete for survival.

So, where does that leave me? I have realised that the question is not just about vegetarian or non-vegetarian. It is about what I truly believe about food and my relationship with it.

Do I believe in minimizing harm? Do I see eating as a personal necessity or a moral responsibility? Is my food choice about taste, or is it about something deeper?

Beyond belief systems, how does my body react to different foods? Some people thrive on plant-based diets, while others feel weaker without animal protein. Some foods energize me, while others make me sluggish.

Much of what I eat has been shaped by my upbringing. If I were born in a different family, would I eat the same way? Do I choose my diet consciously, or am I simply following tradition?

Am I eating for nourishment, or am I eating for comfort? Do I listen to my hunger, or do I eat because of social habits and emotional cravings?

Food as Comfort, Food as Escape

At times, food became my refuge. When I was stressed, I turned to comfort food. When I was bored, I snacked. When I was sad, I indulged in sweets. Food was not just about physical nourishment - it became an emotional escape.

But food is a temporary distraction. It provides relief in the moment, but it does not change the circumstances that led me to seek comfort in the first place. If I eat because I am stressed, the stress does not disappear. If I eat because I am lonely, the loneliness remains.

I have eaten not because my body needed fuel, but because my mind sought comfort. And the more I relied on food for emotional relief, the harder it became to recognize when I was truly hungry.

The Influence of Society on What I Eat

Beyond my emotions, my eating habits have been shaped by the world around me. Society dictates what is considered "healthy" and "unhealthy," "good" and "bad." Food trends come and go - one year, fat is the enemy; the next, it is sugar. A diet once believed to be ideal is later criticized as harmful.

I have also been conditioned to associate food with morality. Eating too much is seen as indulgence; eating too little is seen as discipline. Some foods are labelled as "guilty pleasures," as if eating them requires justification.

And then there is the pressure of how food is presented. Meals are no longer just for sustenance - they are curated for social media, arranged for appearance rather than nourishment. Eating is no longer just a personal experience; it is a public statement.

How much of my diet is truly my choice, and how much is influenced by the world around me?

The Fear of Scarcity and the Habit of Overeating

There have been times when I ate more than I needed - not because I was hungry, but because I feared I might not have food later. Sometimes this was due to upbringing, where finishing everything on my plate was seen as a virtue. Other times, it was an unconscious reaction to an ingrained fear of scarcity.

Even when food is abundant, the fear of "not having enough" lingers. It drives people to eat beyond their needs, to stockpile groceries, to seek security in full plates and full refrigerators.

But food security is not the same as food excess. Eating more than my body requires does not protect me from future hunger. It only weighs me down in the present.

Recognizing this fear has allowed me to reframe my approach to eating - not as something driven by scarcity, but as something to be experienced in balance.

Mindful Eating: Listening to My Body

If my relationship with food has been shaped by emotions, culture, and fear, then how do I return to what is truly natural?

The answer is simple: I must listen to my body. I must eat when I am hungry, not when I am bored, stressed, or pressured. I must stop when I am satisfied, not when my plate is empty or when social norms dictate it. I must choose food that nourishes me, not food that is dictated by trends or guilt.

Eating should not be an unconscious act. Every bite is an opportunity to reconnect with what my body truly needs.

When I eat mindfully, I do not just consume - I experience. I taste, I feel, I appreciate. Food is no longer just something to be swallowed; it is something to be understood.

What This Means for My Life

Food is not my enemy, nor is it my escape. It is not a reward, nor is it a punishment. It is not a status symbol, nor is it a burden. Food is simply food - a necessity, a joy, and a responsibility.

I no longer eat out of habit, emotion, or fear. I eat because my body needs nourishment. I eat because food is meant to be enjoyed, not worshiped or feared. I still appreciate a good meal, but I no longer use food to fill emotional gaps. I still enjoy special dishes, but I no longer let food define my self-worth.

And in this shift, I find balance - not in deprivation, not in indulgence, but in awareness.

Chapter 11

Clothing, Fashion, and Appearance – Expression, Expectation, or Necessity?

Every day, I make choices about how I present myself to the world. Some days, I carefully select what to wear, matching colours, fabrics, and accessories. Other days, I dress with little thought, simply covering my body with whatever is convenient. Yet, no matter what I wear, my clothing, my appearance, and even the way I groom myself become a statement - whether I intend it or not.

At its core, clothing serves a basic function: protection from the elements. But over time, it has evolved into something much more - an expression of identity, a reflection of status, a tool of self-presentation, and in some cases, a professional necessity. Fashion takes it a step further, shaping how I perceive myself and how others perceive me. Even makeup, jewellery, and hairstyles are not just aesthetic choices; they are deeply connected to personal identity, social trends, and professional expectations.

But how much of what I wear and how I present myself is truly my choice? Am I dressing and styling myself for my own comfort and confidence, or am I conforming to external pressures and professional demands? And if clothing is meant to cover me, why does it so often define me?

How My Relationship with Clothing and Appearance Evolved

As a child, I wore what was given to me. I had little control over my clothing or my appearance, and I didn't think much about it. Clothes were simply something to wear, hair was something to comb, and that was enough.

Then, at some point, I realized that the world judged how I looked. Certain outfits brought admiration, while others made me feel invisible. Some styles made me fit in, while others set me apart. I started to care - not just about what I liked, but about how others saw me.

Fashion trends came and went. Some colours were in, some were out. Some body types were considered ideal, others were not. What was once fashionable became outdated. I found myself keeping up, even when I didn't fully understand why.

And then came makeup, grooming, and personal styling - another layer of expectation. Some people wore makeup for confidence, others for social norms. Some kept their appearance simple, while others experimented. I saw how much effort people put into looking a certain way, and I wondered - was it for themselves or for the world?

Clothing and Appearance as Professional Necessity

In certain roles, appearance is not just about self-expression - it is about professional expectations.

A lawyer in court cannot dress casually. A corporate executive cannot show up in pyjamas. A model or television anchor cannot ignore grooming. Even in creative fields, where self-expression is encouraged, there is an unspoken expectation to maintain a presentable look.

Society assigns visual signals to competence. Whether fair or not, dressing well and being well-groomed creates an impression of discipline, reliability, and professionalism. In many workplaces, the way I dress is not just about personal style; it is a requirement for success.

But if professional attire is necessary, does that mean I lose all personal choice? Not necessarily. Even within a dress code, there are ways to maintain individuality without compromising professional decorum.

Instead of seeing formal clothing as a restriction, I can view it as a tool - a way to create a strong presence, to command respect, and to align myself with my work environment. But at the same time, I must be careful not to let external expectations define my entire self-worth.

Clothing as Identity: Self-Expression or Social Expectation?

There is no doubt that clothing and fashion can be empowering. The right outfit can make me feel confident.

A carefully chosen accessory can enhance my mood. A certain style can reflect my personality.

But I must ask - am I choosing my clothing, or has my clothing been chosen for me by society?

Every culture, every era, every social class has its own "rules" for dressing. What is considered appropriate in one place is strange in another. What is seen as beautiful in one era is undesirable in another.

If fashion and beauty standards constantly change, can they really define who I am? Or are they just another way society influences how I see myself?

When I dress a certain way, am I truly expressing myself, or am I following an unspoken rule?

The Illusion of Fashion and Trends

Fashion is a cycle. Every few years, old trends return with a new name. Yesterday's embarrassing style becomes tomorrow's must-have look.

But fashion is not just about clothing - it is an industry built on insecurity. If I am made to feel like my wardrobe is outdated, I will buy more. If I believe that my appearance needs improvement, I will invest in beauty products. If I feel that I need to keep up with trends, I will spend without question.

Trends do not exist to serve me - they exist to keep me consuming. If I stop chasing fashion, does that mean I stop looking good? Or does it mean I finally define style on my own terms?

Makeup, Grooming, and the Beauty Industry

Beauty standards are just as fluid as fashion. What is considered attractive changes from one era to the next. Some cultures favour pale skin, others prefer a tan. Some praise thinness, others admire curves. Even facial features go through cycles of desirability.

And yet, billions are spent every year on beauty products, promising perfection that is impossible to maintain. The industry thrives by making me feel inadequate - by convincing me that I need more products, more enhancements, more effort.

But I must ask: Am I doing this for myself, or am I doing it because I have been told I should? There is nothing wrong with wanting to look good. But when my sense of worth is tied to my appearance, I have lost control. When I need approval for how I look, I am no longer dressing for myself.

How Do I Choose How to Present Myself?

If clothing, fashion, and appearance are both personal and social, then how do I find balance?

I have realized that the key is intention. I must ask myself: Am I dressing or grooming myself in a way that makes me feel good, or am I seeking validation? Does this reflect who I am, or am I afraid of judgment? Do I feel pressured to look a certain way, or am I genuinely comfortable with my choices? Am I following fashion and beauty trends because I enjoy them, or because I feel I must?

The answers are not always simple. But by questioning them, I begin to reclaim my choices.

Letting Go of Appearance as Self-Worth

This does not mean I stop caring about what I wear. It simply means I stop depending on it for self-worth.

I can still appreciate fashion, but I no longer feel defined by it. I can still dress well, but I do not need approval for it. I can still follow trends if I enjoy them, but I do not feel incomplete without them.

I do not have to prove anything through my appearance. I do not have to seek validation in fabric, makeup, or hairstyles. I do not have to follow every rule that society sets.

When I stop using clothing and beauty as a way to control how others see me, I start dressing for myself.

What This Means for My Life

Clothing, fashion, and appearance are not just about how I look - they are about how I feel. I no longer use them as a way to seek validation. I no longer allow them to define my worth.

I still follow professional dress codes where necessary, but I do not let them define me beyond my work. I still care about my appearance, but I do it for myself - not for approval.

And in this, I find freedom. I am no longer bound by the need to prove myself through my appearance. I am not my clothes. I am not my beauty. I am not my image. I am simply me.

Chapter 12

Shelter and Security – How Much is Enough?

A roof over my head. A place to return to at the end of the day. A space that is mine, where I can sleep in peace, eat in comfort, and find protection from the outside world. Shelter is one of the most basic human needs. But beyond survival, it is also one of the greatest sources of emotional security, social status, and financial investment.

For some, a home is a sanctuary - a place of comfort, warmth, and belonging. For others, it is a measure of success - a display of wealth, achievement, or social standing. And for many, it is a struggle - something to constantly work for, pay off, or worry about. But how much of my need for shelter is about genuine security, and how much is about expectation? When does shelter become more than just a necessity and turn into an attachment - a source of anxiety, comparison, or burden? And how do I find the balance between having enough and wanting more?

The Purpose of Shelter: A Basic Human Need

At its simplest level, shelter protects me. It shields me from the elements - rain, heat, cold. It keeps me safe from threats, both natural and human. It provides a space where I can rest, recover, and find privacy. Shelter is one of the few things that humans across all times and cultures have sought to create. Whether it is a simple hut, a grand mansion, or an apartment in a crowded city, having a place to call home gives a sense of stability.

Without a home, survival is difficult. But does that mean the size, location, or luxury of my home determines my happiness? If having a home is necessary, does owning a home bring greater peace, or does it create more pressure?

Home as Identity: Why Shelter Becomes More Than Just a Place to Live

A home is more than walls and a roof. It carries memories, emotions, and meaning. It is where I have celebrated joys, faced struggles, and shared moments with loved ones. It is a space that reflects my personality, my habits, and my choices. But at some point, shelter stops being just a place to live and starts becoming a measure of worth.

Society ties home ownership to success. A bigger house, a better location, a prestigious address - these become signs of achievement. When I was younger, I was taught that owning a home was the ultimate goal. I saw people struggle to buy property, sacrificing present comfort for future security. I saw others take on massive loans, believing that a bigger house meant a better life. I watched families equate the size of a home with status and stability, as if where I live defines who I am.

But does a larger home really mean a happier life? Does owning a house truly make me more secure? Or have I been conditioned to believe that more is always better?

The Cost of Shelter: Financial and Emotional Burdens

A home brings comfort, but it also brings responsibility. Buying a house requires money, often borrowed at the cost of years of repayment. Renting provides flexibility but can feel unstable. Maintaining a home requires effort, repairs, and expenses. Moving from one place to another can be an emotional challenge, disrupting routine and familiarity.

I have seen people work endlessly to buy the perfect home, only to spend their lives worrying about paying for it. I have seen others attach so much meaning to their house that it becomes a source of fear - fear of losing it, fear of decline, fear of comparison. At what point does a home bring peace, and at what point does it become a burden?

Security vs. Attachment: How Much Do I Really Need?

The desire for shelter is natural, but when does it become attachment? If I believe that my home defines me, am I truly free? If I constantly seek a bigger or better house, will I ever be satisfied? If I worry about losing what I have, am I really secure?

True security does not come from walls, locks, or property papers. It comes from knowing that no matter where I live, I can adapt. No matter what happens, I can rebuild. When I let go of attachment to the idea that my home must look a certain way, be in a certain place, or meet a certain standard, I start to see it for what it truly is - a place to rest, to find comfort, but not the definition of my life.

Minimalism, Luxury, and the Balance Between the Two

In some philosophies, having less is seen as a path to freedom. Jainism encourages simple living, avoiding excess. Buddhist monks live with minimal possessions, including modest shelter, believing that attachment leads to suffering. On the other hand, many see a beautiful, well-furnished home as a sign of achievement - a reflection of success, stability, and a life well-lived. Many religious traditions celebrate prosperity as a blessing, believing that a good home is a reward for effort.

Neither extreme is right or wrong. The question is: What do I truly need to feel at peace? For some, a small, simple home is enough. For others, a larger space brings joy. The key is awareness - am I seeking more out of necessity or insecurity?

Renting vs. Owning: The Debate of Stability vs. Freedom

There is a long-standing debate over whether owning a home is better than renting. Owning a home offers stability, long-term security, and an asset for the future. Renting offers flexibility, freedom from maintenance costs, and fewer financial commitments.

Some people feel at peace only when they own a home. Others feel trapped by the burden of ownership. So, which is better? The truth is - it depends on what gives me peace. If I buy out of fear, am I truly secure? If I rent but live in uncertainty, am I truly free? There is no universal answer - only the choice that aligns with what I value most.

How Do I Find Balance?

If shelter is a need, and housing is a responsibility, then how do I find balance? I have started asking myself: Am I living in a place that meets my real needs, or am I trying to impress others? Do I truly need more space, or am I attached to an idea of success? Am I sacrificing too much for a house, at the cost of my present well-being? Does my home give me peace, or does it create stress and anxiety?

The answers guide me toward balance - where I have enough, but not so much that it controls me.

Letting Go of the Illusion of Security

A house can be bought, but security cannot. A home can give comfort, but true stability comes from within. I no longer see shelter as a measure of my success. I do not need the biggest house to feel important. I do not need an expensive address to feel worthy. I do not need to compare my home to someone else's to find happiness.

I still value a comfortable home, but I no longer attach my identity to it. Whether my space is large or small, rented or owned, luxurious or simple - it does not define who I am. I define what home means to me.

What This Means for My Life

Shelter is necessary, but I do not need to burden myself with society's expectations of what my home should be. I choose a space that brings me comfort, but I do not let it become a source of anxiety.

I no longer compare my home to others. I no longer believe that bigger is always better. I no longer live in fear of losing what I have.

I have stopped chasing security in walls and started finding stability within myself. And in this, I finally feel at home.

Chapter 13

Health – The Anchor of My Existence

Health is the foundation upon which everything in life is built. Without it, wealth loses value, success becomes meaningless, and even relationships suffer. A strong body allows me to move through life with energy, a clear mind helps me make wise decisions, and a stable emotional state lets me experience joy and resilience. Beyond all of this, spiritual health gives me the ability to see life with clarity, reducing suffering and attachment.

For most of my life, I have thought about health only when I lost it. When I fell sick, I realized the importance of my body. When I felt anxious, I noticed the chaos in my mind. When I lacked motivation, I saw how intellectual stagnation affected me. But why should health be something I notice only when it fails? Why do I focus on curing problems rather than preventing them?

This chapter is about understanding health in its entirety - not just physical fitness, but also mental, intellectual, and spiritual well-being. True health is not just about avoiding disease; it is about living fully, with awareness and balance.

Physical Health: The Body as the Instrument of Experience

The body is the vessel through which I experience life. Every moment of joy, every struggle, every connection I make happens through my physical form. But do I treat my body with the respect it deserves?

I have often taken my health for granted - neglecting sleep, eating without thought, avoiding movement, and pushing my body to exhaustion. Yet, when my body fails, everything else becomes secondary. A simple illness can make even the most successful person feel powerless.

The body thrives on balance. It does not demand perfection, but it does require care. If I neglect my body, I pay the price later - through fatigue, illness, and limitations. If I obsess over it, I become trapped in another form of attachment. The key is to respect my body, neither worshipping nor ignoring it.

Some simple truths have shaped my understanding of physical health. What I eat determines how I feel. Overindulgence leads to sluggishness, while nourishment brings vitality. A sedentary body stiffens, ages faster, and weakens. Whether through exercise, yoga, or simply walking, the body must move to remain alive. In a world obsessed with productivity, I once believed sleep was a luxury. But I have learned that recovery is just as important as action. The body speaks to me - through fatigue, through discomfort, through energy levels. When I listen, I prevent small problems from becoming major illnesses.

Health is not about looking a certain way. It is not about extreme discipline or pushing myself beyond limits. It is simply about caring for the one thing that allows me to experience this world - the body.

Mental Health: The Stability of the Mind

If the body is the instrument, the mind is the player. A healthy body alone is not enough; my mind determines how I experience life. A restless, anxious, or negative mind can create suffering, even when everything in life is going well.

Mental health is often ignored until it becomes a crisis. But I have learned that mental well-being is not something that happens on its own - it must be cultivated. The way I think, the way I process emotions, and the way I respond to challenges all shape my mental state.

What does a healthy mind need? I am not my thoughts. My mind produces thousands of thoughts daily, but not all of them are true. I do not have to believe everything I think. Anger, fear, and sadness are natural, but when they control me, they consume me. Understanding emotions rather than suppressing them helps me stay balanced. The modern world thrives on stress. But stress is not a sign of importance - it is often a sign of misalignment. A well-balanced life does not require constant tension. Many of my worries come from caring too much about how others see me. A mentally strong person finds validation within, not from approval outside.

If I am constantly reacting to life rather than responding to it with clarity, my mental health is suffering. Just as I train my body, I must train my mind - to be still, to be present, and to be free from unnecessary suffering.

Intellectual Health: The Growth of Understanding

Beyond mental and physical health, there is intellectual well-being - the ability to think critically, learn continuously, and remain open to new perspectives. A stagnant mind leads to boredom, frustration, and rigidity. If I stop learning, I stop growing. If I stop questioning, I become trapped in fixed beliefs. Intellectual health is not about accumulating knowledge, but about keeping my mind sharp, curious, and adaptable.

How do I cultivate intellectual well-being? Expanding my mind with books, experiences, and new ideas keeps me engaged with life. If I never question what I think I know, I remain limited by my conditioning. Growth happens when I dare to be wrong and learn something new. Intelligence is not about knowing everything; it is about realizing how much there is still to learn.

A healthy mind does not seek certainty - it embraces curiosity. The moment I think I know everything, I have stopped growing.

Spiritual Health: The Search for Meaning and Connection

Beyond the body, beyond the mind, beyond even knowledge - there is something deeper. It is the awareness of the infinite self, the realization that "I" am not just my roles, my achievements, or my struggles.

Spiritual health does not mean religious belief. It is simply the ability to see life with perspective. A spiritually healthy person does not get caught up in trivial worries. They are not constantly disturbed by change. They have an inner stability that remains untouched by external circumstances.

How do I cultivate spiritual health? Taking time to question life, existence, and my purpose creates a deeper understanding of the self. A few moments of silence each day remind me that I am not just my thoughts or emotions. If I define myself by what I own, what I do, or how others see me, I will always suffer. Realizing that "I" exist beyond all these things brings peace.

Spiritual well-being is not about escaping life - it is about engaging with it fully while knowing that I am more than my experiences.

How This Connects to the Infinite "I"

Each aspect of health - physical, mental, intellectual, and spiritual - helps me understand the infinite reality of "I." When I see myself only as a body, I become obsessed with appearance and longevity. When I see myself only as a mind, I become lost in emotions and thoughts. When I see myself only as an intellect, I become arrogant.

But when I balance all these aspects, I start seeing life as it truly is. I no longer fear sickness because I respect my body. I no longer fear stress because I have control over my mind. I no longer fear ignorance because I keep learning.

Real health is not just about avoiding illness - it is about living fully, with awareness and balance.

What This Means for My Life

I do not take my health for granted. I do not see my body, mind, or intelligence as separate - I nurture them together. I do not obsess over health out of fear, but I care for it with respect. I strive to live each day with clarity, energy, and presence.

And in doing so, I realize that true well-being is not about merely surviving - it is about thriving, with complete awareness and balance.

Chapter 14

Education, Knowledge, and the Search for Truth

From the moment I could understand words, I was taught that education is the key to success. I was told that knowledge would give me power, respect, and stability. Learning was never presented as a choice - it was a necessity, a step toward a better future. But as I grew older, I began to wonder: what is education really for? Is it just a means to an end, or is there something deeper to it?

For years, I studied because I was expected to. I memorized facts, passed exams, and obtained degrees. I believed that formal education would prepare me for life. But as I stepped out of the classroom, I realized that real learning did not always come from books, and intelligence was not measured by certificates. There was knowledge beyond textbooks, wisdom beyond school, and truths that no institution could teach.

What does it really mean to be educated? Is it about degrees, or is it about understanding the world? Does knowledge make me wiser, or does it sometimes fill me with false confidence? And most importantly, is education truly about freedom, or has it become just another system of control?

The Purpose of Education: A Tool for Growth or a System of Control?

Education is one of the most powerful forces in human life. It shapes how I think, how I see the world, and how I interact with others. A well-educated society thrives on innovation, progress, and wisdom. Education can uplift the poor, challenge outdated beliefs, and open doors to opportunities.

But while education is meant to liberate, it is often used to confine. The modern education system is designed not just to teach, but to standardize. Instead of encouraging curiosity, it often rewards obedience. Instead of fostering creativity, it promotes conformity. Instead of teaching me how to think, it teaches me what to think.

From childhood, I was taught to follow a syllabus, to memorize and repeat, to compete for grades. But what about the questions that do not fit neatly into an exam paper? What about the lessons that cannot be measured? Does education truly encourage knowledge, or does it sometimes suppress it?

Degrees vs. Intelligence: The Myth of Academic Success

In society, degrees are seen as proof of intelligence. A highly educated person is respected, a degree-holder is valued, and academic success is equated with competence. But is that always true?

I have met people with impressive qualifications who struggle to think beyond their training. I have also met people with little formal education who possess deep wisdom. Knowledge and intelligence are not the same thing. A person can be well-read yet lack insight. A person can be uneducated yet deeply wise.

Yet, the world rewards degrees, not wisdom. Jobs are given based on qualifications, not on understanding. Respect is given to those with prestigious backgrounds, even if their thinking is rigid. This creates a false belief - that without formal education, one is less capable, less knowledgeable, less valuable.

But history tells a different story. Some of the greatest minds - people who changed the world - were not products of traditional education. Socrates, Leonardo da Vinci, Ramanujan, and even the Buddha did not conform to an institutional system of learning. Their knowledge came from deep curiosity, questioning, and a search for truth.

So, if education is meant to enlighten, why does it sometimes limit perspective? If intelligence is about curiosity, why does the system focus on memorization?

Knowledge vs. Wisdom: The Difference That Matters

There is a difference between knowing something and understanding it. I can memorize facts about the universe, but does that mean I grasp its mysteries? I can read about kindness, but does that mean I practice it? I can learn about life from books, but does that mean I know how to live?

True wisdom does not come from collecting information - it comes from experiencing, questioning, and reflecting. The world is full of educated people who lack wisdom, and wise people who lack formal education.

I have seen people with knowledge but no humility, intelligence but no kindness, degrees but no real understanding of life. What good is knowledge if it does not make me a better person? What is the purpose of learning if it does not lead to wisdom?

Real education is not about filling my mind - it is about expanding my awareness.

The Role of Curiosity: Learning Beyond the System

Some of the most important things I have learned were never taught in a classroom. I learned patience from failure. I learned resilience from struggle. I learned empathy from loss. I learned more from observing life than I ever did from a textbook.

True learning happens everywhere - in conversations, in experiences, in moments of silence. Some of the greatest insights have come not from teachers, but from mistakes. Not from lectures, but from self-reflection.

The most valuable lessons are often the ones no one teaches. They are the things I realize when I question the world around me.

Yet, most education systems do not encourage questioning - they encourage acceptance. I was told to respect authority, not challenge it. I was taught to answer questions, not ask my own. But the greatest discoveries in history were made by those who challenged what was accepted, who refused to believe something just because they were told to. If I stop questioning, am I truly learning?

Spiritual and Philosophical Learning: The Education of the Self

There is another kind of knowledge - one that cannot be tested or graded. It is the knowledge of the self, of existence, of what lies beyond the material world. Many ancient traditions, including Hinduism, Buddhism, and other philosophical systems, focus not only on external knowledge, but also on inner wisdom.

The great texts of India - the Upanishads, the Bhagavad Gita, the Buddhist sutras - do not just teach facts. They teach how to see reality, how to understand suffering, how to find inner peace. These teachings emphasize that the highest form of knowledge is not about the outside world, but about the nature of the self.

What good is external knowledge if I do not understand myself? What use is mastering the world if I am a stranger to my own mind? If I memorize the scriptures but do not embody their teachings, am I truly educated?

The Practical Necessity of Formal Education

Despite its flaws, formal education remains the most widely accepted means of acquiring knowledge that translates into financial stability. In a world where qualifications open doors, degrees often serve as a minimum requirement for employment. Without them, opportunities become scarce, and financial independence becomes a harder struggle.

Education systems, for all their rigid structures, equip individuals with foundational skills - literacy, numeracy, critical thinking, and problem-solving. A doctor, an engineer, a scientist, or even an artist often needs structured learning before they can practice their craft at a professional level. While some may argue that the truly great minds - Socrates, Ramanujan, or the Buddha - were not shaped by traditional education, the reality for most people is different. Employers, institutions, and even society itself use degrees as a measure of competence.

Rejecting formal education entirely is neither practical nor wise. The key is to use it as a tool rather than an identity. A degree can provide a foundation, but it should not define intelligence or wisdom. Education should be seen to acquire financial security, not as an indicator of one's worth. The real challenge is balancing formal education with self-driven learning - seeking skills for survival while also cultivating knowledge for deeper understanding.

How Do I Choose What to Learn?

If education is both a tool for progress and a system of control, how do I approach it wisely? I cannot reject learning, but I must learn consciously.

Formal education is necessary - it provides the structure, qualifications, and credibility required to navigate the world. It opens doors to financial stability, equips me with essential skills, and allows me to participate meaningfully in society. But it is not enough on its own. True learning goes beyond degrees; it is about curiosity, adaptability, and the ability to think for myself.

I have started asking myself: Am I learning merely to meet expectations, or because I seek understanding? Does this knowledge serve a practical purpose, or does it also help me grow? Am I acquiring skills just for a livelihood, or am I also exploring knowledge that brings deeper meaning to my life?

When I approach learning this way, I do not reject education - I redefine it. I embrace what is useful while recognizing its limitations. I take what serves me and leave behind what confines me. I remain open to knowledge, but I do not allow it to dictate my sense of self-worth.

What This Means for My Life

I no longer see education as just a means to an end, nor do I equate degrees with intelligence. I respect formal learning for the opportunities it provides, but I do not let it define me. True education is not about collecting credentials; it is about developing the ability to think critically, adapt, and find meaning beyond textbooks.

I continue to read, question, and explore. I seek truth not just in classrooms, but in lived experiences. I choose to educate myself not just in facts, but in wisdom - the kind that cannot be tested, graded, or confined to a syllabus.

And in doing so, I finally find freedom - not in what I have been taught, but in the knowledge, I choose to pursue, the understanding I cultivate, and the meaning I create for myself.

Chapter 15

Work, Ambition, and the Pursuit of Success

For most of my life, work has been more than just a means to earn a living- it has shaped my sense of self, measured my worth, and determined my place in society. From an early age, I was told that hard work leads to success and that success brings happiness. But as I moved through life, I began questioning: What exactly is success? Does achieving it guarantee fulfilment?Work is essential. It provides financial stability, structure, and purpose. It allows me to contribute to society, build something of value, and support myself and my family. Yet, I have also seen how work can become a burden - an endless cycle of competition, pressure, and expectation.

There have been moments when I have loved what I do, where work has given me meaning and excitement. And there have been moments when I have felt exhausted, questioning whether this is all there is to life. Do I work to live, or do I live to work? How do I balance ambition with well-being? And if I do not chase success in the way society expects, does that mean I have failed?

The more I have examined my relationship with work, the more I have realized that work is not just one thing - it plays multiple roles in my life. It is about survival, identity, ambition, stability, and purpose. But does it have to define me entirely?

Work as Survival – A Basic Necessity

At its most fundamental level, work is about survival. It provides the resources I need to secure food, shelter, healthcare, and other essentials. No matter how passionate or ambitious I am, I cannot ignore this reality. Without financial stability, even the most meaningful pursuits become difficult.

Yet, I have also seen that when survival becomes the only focus, work can feel like an endless trap. I have met people who work tirelessly, postponing happiness for a future that never arrives. Their entire identity revolves around their income, and the fear of financial loss consumes them.

But even more striking is the fact that not all work is financially compensated. There are millions of people - especially women - who spend their lives working without receiving a paycheque. Running a home, raising children, caring for aging parents, managing households - these are all forms of work, yet they remain largely invisible in economic terms.

I have known women who work longer hours than professionals in offices, yet their contributions are not recognized as "real work." Society defines work narrowly, valuing paid labour over unpaid labour, even though one cannot exist without the other. If financial compensation is the only way work is valued, then what does that say about the countless hours of effort put into caregiving and homemaking?

Work as Identity – Am I My Job?

At some point in my life, work stopped being just a necessity and became a definition of who I am. The question "What do you do?" is not just about my profession - it is an inquiry into my identity.

For many, a job is a source of pride and purpose. It provides confidence, social respect, and a sense of accomplishment. But what happens when a job is lost? If I define myself solely by my career, then when my career disappears, so does my sense of self.

I have met individuals who lost their jobs after decades of dedication to a single company. Overnight, they were no longer "managers," "executives," or "directors." They were just people, stripped of the labels they had worn for years. Some found new opportunities, reinventing themselves with time. Others struggled, their confidence shattered, feeling as though they had lost their purpose.

This is even more striking in the case of those whose work is unpaid - homemakers, caregivers, and those who support others in invisible ways. Their identity is often shaped not by their personal aspirations but by the roles they fulfil in their family and community. When their caregiving responsibilities change - when children grow up, when elderly parents pass away - they may feel a deep void, as though the work that defined them has disappeared.

Work can be a source of meaning, but it should never be the sole measure of who I am. My identity must be bigger than my career or my responsibilities.

The Definition of Success: Mine or Society's?

Success means different things to different people. To some, it is wealth. To others, it is power. Some seek knowledge, some seek creativity, and some seek freedom. Society tells me that success means climbing higher, earning more, achieving more. But is that my definition, or have I simply accepted what I was told?

I have seen individuals who reached the top of their careers only to realize they sacrificed their health, relationships, and peace of mind in the process. I have also seen people who live modestly but feel deeply fulfilled.

If I strip away society's expectations, what does success look like to me? Is it a prestigious job? A simple life with financial independence? A career that allows creativity? A balance between work and personal time?

If I am constantly chasing something, will I ever be satisfied? Or will I always believe that real happiness is just one more achievement away? Perhaps the real challenge is not choosing between ambition and peace - but finding a way to have both.

The Illusion of Job Security and the Fear of Change

For a long time, I believed that a stable job meant a secure future. The world around me reinforced this belief - parents, teachers, and society encouraged me to find a good job, hold onto it, and build my life around it. A steady paycheque, a well-defined career path, and long-term employment were seen as signs of success. But over time, I began to see that true security does not come from a job - it comes from adaptability.

The reality is that no job is truly secure. Companies evolve, industries collapse, technology advances, and economic downturns happen. Even the most loyal employees, those who have dedicated decades to an organization, can find themselves laid off due to corporate restructuring or automation. I have seen highly skilled professionals lose their jobs overnight due to circumstances completely beyond their control. The promise of lifelong employment, once the foundation of financial security, is now increasingly uncertain.

Yet, despite knowing this, the thought of losing a job is terrifying. Why? Because for many, a job is more than just a paycheque - it is an identity, a routine, a sense of purpose. The fear of job loss is not just about financial instability; it is about losing a part of who I am. Without my job title, without my work responsibilities, who am I?

This fear often leads people to cling to jobs they dislike simply because they feel they have no other choice. I have seen individuals stay in toxic workplaces, endure excessive stress, or sacrifice their well-being just because the unknown seems riskier than the misery they already know. "The devil known is better than the devil unknown" - but is that really true?

On the other hand, I have also met people who lost their jobs unexpectedly but used it as a turning point - a chance to reassess their priorities, develop new skills, or even switch careers entirely. While the transition was difficult, they discovered that losing their job did not mean losing themselves. It forced them to step outside their comfort zone and redefine their idea of security.

Security, I have learned, is not about holding onto a single job forever. It is about developing skills that remain relevant regardless of the job market. It is about financial preparedness - saving, investing, and creating multiple sources of income. And most importantly, it is about building a mindset that is adaptable, resilient, and open to change.

There was a time when I viewed job loss as the worst thing that could happen. Now, I see it as just another chapter in life - not an ending, but a redirection. The world is constantly changing, and the ability to navigate that change is what provides true security. The more I learn, evolve, and adapt, the less I fear the uncertainty of tomorrow. Because in the end, real security is not in the job - it is in me.

Work-Life Balance – Myth or Necessity?

For years, I believed in the concept of work-life balance as something tangible, something I could achieve if I just planned my time well enough. But as I moved forward in life, I realized that the line between work and life is not as clear as it seems. Work and personal life are not two separate things that can be neatly divided into equal halves - they constantly influence each other. If I am exhausted from work, I carry that exhaustion into my home. If I am dealing with personal stress, it affects my performance at work. The idea that I can simply "switch off" one when I step into the other is unrealistic.

The modern world, with its constant connectivity, has made this balance even more elusive. Technology has blurred the boundaries between work and personal life. There was a time when leaving the office meant leaving work behind. Now, emails, messages, and deadlines follow me home, demanding my attention even in moments meant for relaxation. I have seen people take work calls during family dinners, reply to emails while on vacation, and struggle to detach from the pressure of being constantly available. The expectation to "always be on" creates a silent anxiety that never fully allows me to rest.

On the other hand, work-life balance is not just about reducing work hours - it is about creating mental and emotional boundaries. I have learned that balance does not necessarily mean working less but working more intentionally. It means knowing when to give my all to work and when to step back and prioritize my well-being. It means understanding that taking breaks is not laziness but a necessary reset for long-term productivity.

At the same time, work-life balance looks different for everyone. For some, their work is their passion, and they willingly pour in long hours without feeling drained. For others, work is just a job - a means to an end - and they find fulfilment in other areas of life. The challenge is not to define balance based on external standards, but to find what balance means for me personally.

I have also come to understand that balance is not always about time distribution but about energy distribution. There are times when work demands more from me - tight deadlines, important projects, career transitions. But just as I dedicate myself to work when required, I must also dedicate time to myself when needed. If I do not make time for my relationships, my hobbies, my health, and my personal growth, I will eventually burn out.

Perhaps the greatest lesson I have learned about work-life balance is that it is not a fixed state - it is a constant adjustment. Some phases of life demand more work, while others allow for more personal time. Rather than aiming for a rigid "50-50" split, I have learned to stay flexible, listen to my needs, and create space for both ambition and rest.

Ultimately, the goal is not to simply balance work and life but to integrate them in a way that allows me to succeed in my career without sacrificing my well-being. Because at the end of the day, no amount of professional success will matter if I am too exhausted to enjoy the life, I have worked so hard to build.

Work as a Chapter, Not the Whole Story

I no longer see work - whether in a formal career or in the unpaid labour of daily life - as the end goal of life. It is an important chapter, but it is not the whole book.

I will work to survive, to grow, to contribute. I will give my best without letting my job define me. I will remain open to change, rather than fearful of it. I will recognize that all work has value - whether it is recognized or not, whether it is paid or not, whether it is inside an office or inside a home.

Work matters, but life is bigger than work. And as long as I am aware of that, I will never lose myself in the job I do - I will always remember who I am beyond it.

Chapter 16

Money and Wealth – Freedom or Illusion?

Like most of us, I have also been told that money is essential. I need it to survive, to live comfortably, to secure my future. Money is a source of power, a measure of success, and the foundation of stability. Without it, everything becomes a struggle. With it, life becomes easier.

But I have also seen how money consumes people. The desire for wealth never truly ends. No matter how much I earn, there is always more to chase. I have seen people sacrifice their health, their relationships, and their peace of mind in pursuit of financial success. I have met individuals who are wealthy beyond measure, yet constantly anxious about losing what they have.

What role should money play in my life? Is it simply a tool, or has it become an obsession? Does financial security bring true freedom, or does it trap me in an endless cycle of greed and fear? And most importantly, how much is enough?

The Purpose of Money: Security, Comfort, and Opportunity

Money is not evil. It is neither good nor bad - it is simply a tool. It allows me to buy food, pay for shelter, and afford healthcare. It gives me the freedom to make choices, to pursue opportunities, to help those I care about. Without money, even basic survival becomes difficult.

In a world where everything is tied to finances, having enough money brings peace of mind. It provides security in times of crisis, a safety net when things go wrong. It allows me to live with dignity, to care for my family, and to plan for the future.

But when does enough turn into never enough? If I have food on my table, a roof over my head, and the ability to meet my needs, why do I still desire more?

The Illusion of Wealth: When Money Controls Me

The world glorifies wealth. People admire the rich, aspire to their lifestyles, and measure success by bank balances. From childhood, I was taught that financial success is the ultimate goal - that being wealthy means I have *made it in life*. Yet, I have seen how money creates its own prison.

Some people, despite having everything, live in fear - fear of loss, fear of competition, fear of not having enough. Their wealth does not bring peace; it brings anxiety. Their money does not free them; it binds them to an endless cycle of earning, accumulating, and protecting.

If wealth truly brings happiness, why do so many rich people feel empty? If money solves all problems, why do billionaires still suffer from stress, loneliness, and insecurity?

The truth is, money can buy comfort, but it cannot buy contentment. It can provide options, but it cannot create inner peace. The more I attach my happiness to wealth, the more I become dependent on something that is never stable.

Greed, Fear, and the Trap of More

At what point does ambition turn into greed? Where does financial security end, and obsession begin?

Greed does not always look like corruption or exploitation. Sometimes, it looks like a constant desire for more, even when I already have enough. It looks like comparing my wealth to others', feeling inadequate despite having plenty. It looks like sacrificing my present for a future that never seems secure enough.

Fear plays a huge role in how I view money. What if something happens tomorrow? What if I need more? What if I fall behind? I have worked so hard - what if it all disappears? If I do not appear successful, will people respect me?

These fears are not based on reality - they are based on attachment to money as my source of security. But no amount of wealth can guarantee safety from life's uncertainties. True security comes not from how much I have, but from knowing I can adapt to whatever happens.

The Balance Between Earning and Living

Money is important. Financial independence is empowering. But if my entire life revolves around earning, when do I start living? I have met people who have spent decades chasing wealth, only to realize too late that they missed out on time with their loved ones, on moments of joy, on simple pleasures that money cannot replace.

I do not want to wake up one day and realize that I spent my entire life accumulating wealth, only to die with regrets. If money is a tool, then I must use it wisely - to create stability, to support experiences, to enable a meaningful life. This does not mean I stop working hard. It does not mean I reject financial success. It simply means I do not let money define me.

When Is Money Enough?

How do I know when I have enough? This question has no simple answer, because society always tells me I need more. If I earn a certain amount, I start believing I need twice as much. If I buy a house, I want a bigger one. If I reach one milestone, another appears. But the truth is, enough is a mindset, not a number.

If I can meet my needs, live comfortably, and plan for the future, why should I feel that I need more? If my wealth does not add to my happiness, why am I still chasing it? Some people live happily with little. Others are miserable despite having everything. The difference is not in their wealth - it is in their relationship with money.

Wealth and Giving: The Power of Sharing

Money has the power to change lives, not just mine but others'. Some of the greatest joy I have experienced is not in earning money, but in using it for something meaningful. When I share my wealth - whether through charity, helping loved ones, or contributing to a cause - it shifts my focus from accumulation to contribution. Instead of seeing money as something to hoard, I see it as something to circulate, to empower, to uplift.

Many spiritual traditions emphasize detachment from money. Hinduism speaks of *daan* (giving without expectation), Buddhism teaches *simplicity*, and even modern financial wisdom acknowledges that hoarding wealth does not create happiness - using it wisely does. This does not mean I must give away all that I have. But it does mean I must see money not as an end, but as a means to something greater.

How Do I Approach Money Wisely?

If money is both essential and dangerous, how do I handle it wisely? The key is balance.

I must learn to earn enough to meet my needs and secure my future, but not at the cost of my well-being. I must save wisely, but not live in constant fear of financial insecurity. I must invest in experiences, relationships, and personal growth, not just in material possessions. I must detach from money as my only source of security and identity.

Money is important, but it is not everything. If I can buy what I need, if I have security for the future, if I can support my family and enjoy my life - then I have enough.

What This Means for My Life

I no longer see money as my master. I do not chase wealth endlessly, believing that more will bring happiness. I work hard, but I do not let work consume my life. I earn wisely, but I do not let fear dictate my financial choices.

I remind myself that money is a tool, not a purpose. It should serve me, not control me. At the end of my life, I will not measure my worth by how much money I had, but by how well I lived. True wealth is not in my bank account - it is in my experiences, my relationships, my peace of mind. And in understanding this, I finally feel free.

This Page has been intentionally left Blank

In the mirrors of relationships, responsibilities, and unspoken desires, the 'I' often loses itself in roles it did not choose. Yet behind every connection, every success, and every longing, there remains a self, waiting to be seen—not through others, but through the silence within.

Section IV

Relationships, Roles and Desire

Chapter 17

Relationships – Connections, Attachments and Letting Go

From the moment I was born, I was not alone. My life has always been intertwined with others - family, friends, mentors, colleagues, even strangers I barely remember. These relationships have shaped me in ways I did not always realize. Some provided warmth, some taught hard lessons, and some left lasting imprints long after they were gone.

I have played many roles in these relationships - child, sibling, friend, partner, colleague, mentor, and sometimes even a stranger to those who once meant everything to me. Relationships, I have come to see, are not fixed. They evolve, shift, and, at times, disappear. And yet, they are among the most powerful forces that define the "I" I have built over time.

But what does it mean to have relationships? Do they exist to fulfil me? Do they complete me? Or are they merely reflections of my inner world, teaching me about myself?

Family: The First Mirror of My Identity

My earliest understanding of relationships came from my family. They were the first people I saw, the first voices I

124

heard, the first hands that held me. In many ways, family is where I first learned who I was.

Family roles often come with expectations - some spoken, some unspoken. As a child, I was expected to obey, to learn, to grow into someone my parents could be proud of. As I got older, I saw that family is not just about receiving care but also about giving it.

There is an emotional paradox within family relationships. They provide a sense of belonging, yet sometimes, they also confine us with obligations and traditions that may not always align with our evolving selves. My relationship with my family has not been static. It has changed as I have changed. The people who once guided me now sometimes seek my guidance. The hands that held me up when I was weak now need my support as they grow older.

Family, in its truest form, is not about obligation but about understanding, acceptance, and adaptation. Yet, I have learned that even family relationships need boundaries - not as walls, but as spaces where both love and individuality can coexist.

Friendship: Chosen Bonds, Evolving Connections

Unlike family, which I was born into, friendships are bonds I have chosen. Some friendships lasted decades, some faded naturally, and some ended in ways I never expected.

I have had friendships that lifted me, where conversations flowed effortlessly, where I felt seen and understood without having to explain myself. But I have also had friendships where expectations became burdens, where closeness turned into dependency, or where time simply pulled us apart.

One of the hardest lessons I have learned is that not all friendships are meant to last forever - and that is okay. People grow, priorities change, and sometimes, distance (physical or emotional) is the natural course of a relationship. I used to believe that losing friends was a failure, but now I see it as part of the rhythm of life. Some people walk with me for a short while, some for longer, but no one is meant to walk with me forever.

True friendship, I have realized, is not about permanence - it is about presence. It is about being there when it matters, about sharing experiences, about mutual respect and joy, even if life eventually takes us in different directions.

The Weight and Freedom of Expectations

Every relationship - family, friendship, or otherwise - comes with expectations. Some expectations are natural; others become burdens. There were times when I felt trapped in roles I did not choose, where I was expected to be a certain way, fulfil certain duties, meet certain emotional needs. But as I have grown, I have questioned: Are these expectations truly mine, or are they things I have carried without choice?

The reality is expectations are not the problem - attachment to them is. The moment I believe that a relationship must always be a certain way, I set myself up for suffering. People change, circumstances shift, and clinging to fixed expectations only leads to disappointment.

This does not mean I stop caring or stop showing up for those who matter. It simply means I recognize the changing nature of relationships and learn to navigate them with both commitment and flexibility.

Letting Go: When to Hold On, When to Release

One of the hardest aspects of relationships is knowing when to let go. I have struggled with this - whether in friendships, family ties, or professional relationships. There is always a part of me that resists endings, that wants to hold on to what once was, that fears the void that letting go creates.

But I have learned that letting go does not mean forgetting or abandoning. It means accepting that people grow apart without resentment, allowing relationships to evolve instead of forcing them to remain the same and understanding that endings are not failures - they are natural transitions.

Letting go is not about cutting people off; it is about releasing attachment to what no longer serves the relationship. Sometimes, I have had to let go of my own expectations rather than the person. Other times, I have had to accept that a relationship has run its course.

I have seen that clinging to relationships out of fear - fear of loneliness, fear of change, fear of hurting others - only leads to suffering. When I let go with awareness and grace, I make space for new connections, new experiences, and new growth.

Love Without Attachment: The Balance of Connection

I once believed that deep love meant deep attachment. That if I loved someone - family, friends, a partner - I should never let go, never allow distance, never change the nature of the bond. But now I see that true love allows freedom.

To love without attachment is to give without expecting anything in return, be present without clinging to permanence and care deeply without controlling the other person's journey. This is not detachment in the sense of indifference- it is detachment from possessiveness and fear.

I can love my family while still being my own person. I can cherish friendships while allowing them to evolve. I can build deep connections without the illusion that they will always remain the same. When I stop holding on too tightly, relationships become lighter, more fulfilling, and more authentic.

Relationships as a Reflection of "I"

Every person I have encountered has been a mirror. Some reflected my strengths, some revealed my weaknesses, some taught me lessons I resisted learning. Relationships, I have come to understand, are not just about who they are but also about who I become through them.

The people I love deeply show me my capacity for connection. The people who challenge me reveal where I need to grow. The people I lose teach me about impermanence and acceptance. Relationships are not meant to complete me; they are meant to expand me.

Living and Loving with Awareness

I no longer expect relationships to remain fixed. I no longer believe that love must always mean attachment. And I no longer fear letting go when it is necessary.

Instead, I have chosen to engage in relationships with awareness, presence, and gratitude - to cherish the moments I share with others while understanding that nothing, not even the deepest love, is truly permanent.

This has not made my relationships weaker; it has made them stronger, freer, and more fulfilling. Because when I love without clinging, I do not lose people - I set them free. And in that freedom, I set myself free too.

Chapter 18

Children and Parenthood – An Extension of "I"?

For much of my life, I believed that parenthood was a natural extension of adulthood. It was not just something people did - it was something that defined them. As I grew older, I saw how society reinforced this idea. Parenthood was spoken of as the ultimate fulfilment, the point where "I" becomes "we," and then "we" extends into the next generation." But as I observed more, as I saw the complexities of being a parent, I began to wonder: *Is having children truly an extension of "I"? Or is it the beginning of something entirely different?*

Becoming a parent is often described as a journey of selflessness, yet I have seen that it is also deeply personal. Some people find meaning in raising children, feeling that their existence continues through them. Others see parenthood as an act of responsibility, tradition, or even obligation. And yet, some do not feel the pull toward parenthood at all. This made me question - *do children truly extend the self, or do they challenge the very idea of "self" as we know it?*

Parenthood as an Expansion of Self

The idea that **children are an extension of "I"** is not new. Many philosophies, both Eastern and Western, have suggested that through children, a part of us lives on. In

Advaita Vedanta, the concept of "I" is already seen as something beyond the physical self, yet in the material world, children are often viewed as a continuation of our lineage, our values, and even our genetic identity.

Scientific studies also support this idea in a biological sense. Research in epigenetics suggests that while we pass on genes, environmental and emotional factors also shape how those genes express themselves in our children. In a way, our experiences do not just stay with us - they become imprinted in the next generation. This reinforces the idea that parenthood is not just about raising a child, but about passing on parts of who we are - our fears, our dreams, our lessons. But does this mean that children are simply reflections of us?

The Illusion of Ownership Over Children

One of the hardest truths about parenthood is that while children come from us, they are not us. The idea that they are merely an extension of their parents can create expectations that burden both the parent and the child.

In Kahlil Gibran's *The Prophet*, he writes: *"Your children are not your children. They are the sons and daughters of Life's longing for itself. They come through you but not from you, And though they are with you, yet they belong not to you."*

This wisdom is echoed in psychology as well. Studies in child development suggest that children's personalities, interests, and choices are not always shaped by parental influence alone, but also by genetics, social factors, and personal experiences. No matter how much a parent tries to mould a child, they will always have their own distinct path, separate from their parents' expectations.

Yet, letting go of this idea can be difficult. Many parents place their unfulfilled dreams, hopes, and even fears onto their children, hoping that they will carry forward what they could not achieve. This can create tension and disappointment when children choose a path different from what was envisioned for them.

I have seen parents who struggled to accept that their children were not mirrors of themselves. And I have seen children who carried the silent burden of trying to be what their parents wanted them to be. This made me question - what if true parenthood is not about extension, but about allowing the child to unfold into their own "I"?

The Responsibility of Parenthood: A Role, Not an Identity

Being a parent is undoubtedly a profound responsibility. Unlike other relationships, where both people enter by choice, parenthood begins with a fundamental asymmetry - a child does not choose to be born. This places a deep ethical responsibility on parents. But where does this responsibility end?

Many parents believe that they must protect, guide, and provide - but beyond a certain point, does responsibility turn into control? Research in autonomy-supportive parenting suggests that the healthiest children are those whose parents allow them independence while providing emotional security. Overparenting, or trying to dictate every aspect of a child's life, often results in anxiety and dependency rather than resilience.

This made me reconsider the idea of parenthood as identity. Many parents define themselves entirely through their children. Their happiness, purpose, and even social standing are tied to how successful their children become. But what happens when children grow up and make choices that do not align with their parents' values? If a child rejects a tradition, a career path, or even a belief system, does it mean the parent has failed?

I have come to see that parenthood is a role, not a permanent identity. The greatest act of parenthood may not be shaping a child, but knowing when to step back, when to let go, and when to trust that the child is capable of creating their own life.

Do We Owe Our Parents for Giving Us Life?

If children are not extensions of their parents, then a question arises - *do we owe our parents for giving us life?* Many cultures, particularly in India, China, and Japan, emphasize filial duty, the idea that children must care for and honour their parents as a moral obligation. In contrast, Western societies lean more toward individual autonomy, where children are not bound to repay their parents for their upbringing.

Philosophically, this raises an interesting dilemma. Does the act of giving life create a permanent debt? The Confucian perspective would argue that yes, parents sacrifice for their children, and thus, children must reciprocate that care. But existentialist thinkers like Simone de Beauvoir would argue that no person chooses to be born, so they cannot be indebted for a choice they did not make.

In my own reflections, I have come to believe that while gratitude toward parents is natural, guilt should not be the foundation of a parent-child relationship. True love between a parent and child should be a choice, not an obligation. Parents who expect love as a return on investment create relationships based on duty rather than genuine care.

What This Means for My Life

I no longer see children as an extension of "I", but as a life that passes through me, shaped by me, but ultimately distinct from me. Parenthood is not about ownership, nor about fulfilling incomplete dreams. It is about creating space for another human being to become their own "I."

I recognize that parenthood, like any responsibility, must be carried without attachment to outcome. I can guide, I can teach, I can nurture - but ultimately, the child must live their own life.

At the same time, as a child, I do not see my life as something I "owe" my parents. Gratitude is different from obligation. Love should not be repaid like a debt - it should flow naturally, without coercion.

Parenthood is perhaps the greatest test of detachment, of love without control, and of care without possession. When I understand this, I do not see children as an extension of "I", but as another life that I am privileged to witness, nurture, and ultimately set free.

Chapter 19

Responsibility Without Burden

For much of my life, I was taught that responsibility was a duty - something I had to carry, a weight I could not set down. Being responsible meant doing what was expected of me, ensuring that I met my obligations, and not failing those who relied on me. Responsibility was not a choice; it was a necessity, a mark of maturity and reliability.

But as I lived, I began to notice something troubling. The more responsibilities I took on, the heavier they became. With every commitment, I felt the pressure of doing things perfectly. I carried the weight of my career, my relationships, my family obligations, my financial security - all at once. At times, responsibility felt like a burden rather than an empowering choice. Instead of making me feel capable, it made me feel trapped.

And so, I started questioning the stories I told myself about responsibility. What if responsibility was not meant to weigh me down? What if I could fulfil my obligations without feeling overwhelmed? What if responsibility, instead of being a burden, could be a source of strength and fulfilment?

Responsibility as a Privilege, Not a Punishment

For a long time, I viewed responsibility as something imposed upon me - by family, by society, by my own circumstances. But then, I began to see it differently.

Responsibility is not just an obligation; it is a privilege. It means that I have the ability to respond to life, to shape my experiences, to make choices that matter.

Some people long for responsibility - entrepreneurs who want to build something meaningful, parents who wish to raise a family, leaders who strive to guide others. Responsibility, when viewed correctly, is a sign of agency. It means I am trusted, that my actions have impact. But the key is to carry it without letting it crush me.

This shift in mindset changed everything. Instead of dreading responsibility, I started seeing it as a way to create meaning. Instead of feeling burdened by commitments, I started appreciating that I had people and things in my life that mattered enough to take responsibility for.

The Burden of Over-Responsibility

However, not all responsibility is empowering. Sometimes, I took on responsibilities that were never mine to bear. I felt responsible for people's happiness, for fixing their problems, for ensuring that everything ran smoothly - even when it was beyond my control.

Psychologists call this *over-responsibility* - a tendency to take on more than one should, often at the expense of one's own well-being. Studies suggest that people who internalize excessive responsibility tend to experience higher levels of stress, anxiety, and even burnout. This is particularly true in cultures where responsibility is tied to self-worth.

I began to see this in myself. The weight of being responsible for everything - whether at work, in relationships, or within my family - was unsustainable. I was holding myself accountable for things that were never mine to control.

Letting go of *over-responsibility* did not mean abandoning my commitments. It simply meant understanding the boundaries of my role. I am responsible for my actions, my decisions, my responses to situations. But I am not responsible for how others react, for the choices they make, or for fixing everything that goes wrong. This realization was liberating. It allowed me to fulfill my duties without feeling trapped by them.

Balancing Responsibility and Self-Care

One of the biggest mistakes I made was believing that responsibility and self-care were in conflict. If I was responsible, I thought I had to sacrifice my own well-being. If I took care of myself, I worried that I was being selfish. But research in positive psychology suggests otherwise - people who balance responsibility with self-care are more resilient, more productive, and actually perform better in their obligations.

I began to rethink what it meant to be responsible. Responsibility does not mean martyrdom. It does not mean draining myself to the point of exhaustion. If I burn out, I am of no help to anyone - not to my work, my family, or myself. True responsibility includes taking care of my own well-being, so that I can show up fully for the things that matter.

I started setting boundaries. I started saying no when necessary. I started prioritizing rest, knowing that a well-rested mind makes better decisions than an exhausted one. And I learned that by taking care of myself, I was actually able to be more present and effective in my responsibilities.

Letting Go of the Guilt of Saying No

For a long time, I felt guilty whenever I declined a request, even when I knew I could not handle more. Saying no felt like failing someone, like neglecting my duty. But I soon realized that saying yes to everything meant saying no to myself.

Sociologists have studied the phenomenon of *role overload* - when people take on too many responsibilities at once, leading to stress, dissatisfaction, and even resentment. Learning to say no is not about being selfish; it is about maintaining balance.

When I started saying no to things that were not aligned with my priorities, I found that my yeses became more meaningful. I was more engaged, more committed, more present. And paradoxically, this made me more responsible, not less.

Responsibility Without the Fear of Failure

One of the heaviest aspects of responsibility is the fear of failing. I worried that if I made a mistake, I would disappoint those who depended on me. But when I looked at the people I admired, I noticed something - they, too, had failed.

Responsibility does not mean perfection. It means showing up, doing my best, and learning from the outcomes - whether they are successes or setbacks. Research in growth mindset psychology shows that people who view responsibility as a learning experience rather than a test of worth tend to be more resilient and less prone to burnout (Dweck, 2006).

I stopped seeing responsibility as a pass-fail test. Instead, I started approaching it with curiosity - what can I learn from this? How can I grow from this experience? This shift removed the fear and replaced it with a sense of purpose and engagement.

What This Means for My Life

I no longer see responsibility as a burden, nor do I see it as something to fear. Responsibility is simply the ability to respond to life - to take ownership of my actions, to commit to the things that matter, and to accept what is beyond my control.

I no longer take responsibility for things that are not mine to carry. I no longer let guilt force me into saying yes when I should say no. I no longer believe that responsibility means sacrificing myself. Instead, I see it as an act of choice, a privilege, and a path to fulfilment.

And in doing so, I have found that responsibility, when carried correctly, does not weigh me down. It lifts me up.

Chapter 20

Success, Failure, and the Stories I Tell Myself

For much of my life, I have been taught to chase success and avoid failure. Success was something to be proud of, something that defined my worth, while failure was a stain to be erased as quickly as possible. But as I have lived, I have come to realize that success and failure are not opposites - they are two sides of the same coin, and both are essential parts of my journey.

Success feels good. It brings validation, rewards, and sometimes even a sense of security. But I have also seen that success can create pressure. The more I succeed, the more I am expected to succeed again. The moment I achieve something, the world asks, "What next?" - and suddenly, the joy of success is overshadowed by the weight of maintaining it.

Failure, on the other hand, feels uncomfortable. It brings disappointment, self-doubt, and sometimes even shame. But when I look back, I see that my greatest growth has come not from moments of success, but from my failures. Every time I failed, I learned something - about myself, about life, about resilience. Failure taught me lessons that success never could.

And so, I have begun to question the stories I tell myself about success and failure. What if success is not what I thought it was? What if failure is not a dead end, but simply a bend in the road?

Success: More Than Just Achievement

For the longest time, I believed success was something external - money, status, recognition, or reaching a particular milestone. Society defines success in measurable terms: the job I have, the wealth I accumulate, the things I own. And so, I pursued those markers, believing that achieving them would bring fulfilment.

But when I reached certain goals, I realized that success was not as permanent or satisfying as I had imagined. The excitement of accomplishment would fade, replaced by the pressure of maintaining it or moving on to the next goal. The definition of success kept shifting, making it feel like a race with no finish line.

What I have come to understand is that success is not a fixed destination - it is a state of being. It is not just about reaching goals but about how I feel when I reach them. It is about the alignment between my actions and my values. Some of the most successful moments of my life have not been the ones that brought external rewards but the ones that brought inner fulfilment - a moment of clarity, a meaningful connection, a sense of purpose.

This does not mean ambition is wrong. It simply means that if I define success only by external achievements, I will always feel like I am chasing something, never truly arriving. True success is when my external achievements align with my inner contentment.

Failure: A Redirection, Not a Definition

Failure is painful. It has shaken my confidence, made me question my abilities, and sometimes made me want to give up. But when I reflect on my past failures, I see something interesting - each failure eventually led me somewhere else, somewhere I needed to be.

I have failed at jobs, only to find new opportunities that suited me better. I have failed in relationships, only to discover deeper self-awareness. I have failed in personal goals, only to realize that I was chasing something that did not truly align with me.

Failure is not a statement about my worth - it is simply a signal that something needs to change. Sometimes, failure teaches me persistence. Other times, it tells me to let go and choose a different path. The real suffering comes not from failure itself, but from how I interpret it. If I see failure as a personal flaw, I will feel shame. But if I see failure as feedback, I will learn and grow.

Most of the people I admire have failed - many times. The difference is that they did not let failure define them. They used it as fuel, as information, as a stepping stone to something greater.

The Fear of Failure and the Trap of Success

What is more dangerous: the fear of failure, or the pressure of success? For a long time, I believed failure was my biggest enemy. I avoided risks, played it safe, and did not take opportunities because I feared the pain of failing. But now, I see that the fear of failure is far worse than failure itself. When I avoid failure at all costs, I stop growing. I live within the boundaries of comfort, never pushing beyond what is familiar.

On the other hand, success comes with its own weight. The moment I achieve something, I feel the pressure to maintain it, to surpass it, to prove that it was not a fluke. Success creates expectations - not just from the world, but from myself. I start believing that I cannot afford to fail, and in doing so, I make success a burden rather than a joy.

Neither fear of failure nor obsession with success leads to freedom. The only way to truly succeed is to redefine both. Success is not about avoiding failure, and failure is not the opposite of success. They are both part of a greater journey of learning and becoming.

Letting Go of the Need for Constant Validation

One of the hardest lessons I have learned is that success loses its meaning when it is tied only to validation from others. I have worked hard for things not because I truly wanted them, but because I wanted recognition. I have felt empty after achieving something because I realized I was doing it for approval rather than for myself.

External success is temporary. If my sense of worth depends on how others see me, I will always feel like I need to prove myself. But if my success is defined by my own sense of purpose and fulfilment, it becomes a lasting source of joy.

At the same time, failure loses its sting when I stop seeing it as humiliation and start seeing it as growth. When I stop worrying about how the world perceives my failures, I free myself to take risks, to try, to experiment.

The moment I stop tying my self-worth to success or failure, I become truly free.

What This Means for My Life

I no longer see success as just external achievements, nor do I see failure as a permanent setback. Success, for me, is when my actions align with my values, when I grow as a person, when I find meaning in what I do. Failure is not an identity - it is an experience, a stepping stone, a necessary part of learning.

I do not fear failure anymore, and I do not chase success at the cost of my peace. I pursue excellence, but not at the expense of joy. I embrace ambition, but not at the cost of my well-being.

And in doing so, I realize that success and failure were never about what the world thought of me - they were always about how I chose to see myself.

Chapter 21

Desire, Identity, and the Conditioned Self

Of all human drives, sexuality is among the most powerful. It is deeply personal, yet universally experienced. It is celebrated and suppressed, sacred and taboo, tender and raw - all at once. In Indian society, as in many others, sexuality often remains unspoken, veiled behind modesty, morality, or discomfort. And yet, it plays a profound role in shaping how I perceive myself, how I relate to others, and how I form identity.

From early adolescence, I am introduced to this force not as something neutral, but something heavily loaded - with desire, guilt, curiosity, shame, fantasy, and expectation. It becomes a part of how I define myself: as attractive or unattractive, desired or ignored, masculine, feminine, or something in between. My body becomes more than a vessel of experience - it becomes an object of attention, comparison, or concealment.

But in the quiet of reflection, I must ask: Is this identity rooted in something essential, or is it a product of conditioning?

The Role of Conditioning – How I Learn to Desire

Like so many aspects of my identity, my experience of sexuality is not just biological - it is shaped by culture, media, religion, and family. I am told what is acceptable, what is shameful, what is "normal," and what is not. Desire, instead of being understood, is often judged. Physical attraction is either exaggerated into obsession or muted into repression. Intimacy becomes something I seek externally, hoping it will complete me, validate me, or make me feel whole.

But where did these ideas come from? If I was never told what beauty looks like, would I still desire the same forms? If I was never taught shame, would I still feel guilty for having a body that feels? If I was never praised or judged for sexual attention, would I still define my worth by it?

So much of what I desire has been handed to me, silently shaped by images, beliefs, and silences. And like all conditioning, once I begin to see it clearly, I gain the power to question it.

Pleasure and the Illusion of Fulfilment

There is nothing inherently wrong with pleasure. Like food or music, sensual pleasure can be deeply enriching. But when I mistake pleasure for fulfilment, I get caught in an endless cycle. I seek pleasure, I experience it briefly, and then I seek it again. Each peak leaves me wanting more - not because it was not satisfying, but because I believed it would give me something it could not: lasting peace.

Sexual desire often masquerades as a promise - of connection, of wholeness, of transcendence. And yet, after the moment passes, what remains? Sometimes joy, sometimes emptiness. And often, the return of longing. The problem is not in the act itself, but in the expectation, I place upon it.

If I believe that intimacy with another will resolve the question of who I am, then I am placing my self-worth in something that is always changing - moods, bodies, attention, and time. That expectation becomes a trap, not freedom.

The Infinite "I" and the Role of Desire

In the journey of this book, I have questioned every label that defines me: my name, my work, my thoughts, my roles. Sexual identity, too, is a role - one more mask worn by the ego, one more construct through which I define "I." But what if the true "I" is not bound by desire at all?

This does not mean suppressing or denying sexuality. It means seeing it clearly - not as the essence of who I am, but as one passing wave in the ocean of awareness. The body may feel arousal, the mind may generate fantasy, the heart may seek connection - but the awareness behind all these remains untouched.

The Upanishads speak of Brahman as that which is beyond all dualities - beyond pleasure and pain, attraction and aversion, male and female. To realize the infinite "I" is to see that while I may experience desire, I am not limited by it. I can engage with it consciously, or let it pass. I do not need to reject my humanity - but I also do not need to be enslaved by it.

What This Means for My Life

I no longer treat sexuality as something to be hidden, nor as something that defines my worth. I see it as part of the human experience - powerful, beautiful, and sometimes confusing - but not the totality of who I am. I understand that attraction is natural, but identity is deeper. That longing can arise, but awareness can remain still.

In a world that either exaggerates or silences sexuality, I choose to see it for what it is - a force to be respected, understood, and integrated - not feared or idolized. And in that awareness, I find freedom - not from the experience itself, but from the illusion that it defines me.

This Page has been intentionally left Blank

We all seek meaning. We all ask: why am I here? But beneath goals and ambitions lies a subtler question—what is the purpose of being itself? Let these chapters lead you beyond doing, into a more intimate space of reflection.

Section V

Meaning and Purpose in Life

Chapter 22

Purpose of Life, Purpose in Life

For much of my life, I have questioned my purpose. Sometimes, I felt certain about what I was meant to do. Other times, I felt lost, as if I were drifting without direction. Society told me that my purpose should be clear - achieve success, build a career, start a family, contribute to society. But was that all? Was purpose something external, something to be achieved? Or was it something deeper, something that existed even before I tried to define it?

Some people seem to be born with a clear sense of purpose- artists, scientists, spiritual leaders, athletes. Others spend their lives searching for it. And yet, I have also seen that even those who achieve their greatest ambitions often feel an emptiness that remains. This made me wonder about what purpose is. Is purpose something I find, or something I create? Is it fixed, or does it change as I evolve? And if I never discover my "true purpose," does that mean my life was wasted?

Is the Pursuit of Happiness the Purpose of Life?

For many, happiness seems to be the ultimate goal. The phrase "pursuit of happiness" is woven into modern culture, suggesting that life is about seeking joy and fulfilment. But when I examine it closely, I see a paradox

- the more I chase happiness, the more elusive it becomes.

Happiness is not a constant state. It is fleeting, often dependent on circumstances. I have felt happiness when achieving something, when being with loved ones, when experiencing something new. But I have also noticed that once the moment passes, the happiness fades. If the purpose of life is happiness, then life becomes a constant chase - a pursuit with no permanent destination.

More importantly, if happiness is the purpose, then what happens when suffering arrives? Every life experiences pain - loss, failure, uncertainty. If my only goal is happiness, then suffering becomes something to be avoided rather than something to be understood. And yet, I have learned more from my difficult moments than from my happiest ones.

Perhaps happiness is not the purpose of life, but rather a byproduct of living meaningfully. It arises when I am in alignment with what matters to me, when I am present, when I am engaged in something greater than myself. Happiness may come and go, but meaning remains.

The Difference Between Purpose in Life and the Purpose of Life

I have come to see that there are two different questions I must ask: What is the purpose of life itself? (*A universal, existential question - why does life exist at all?*) and What is my purpose in life? (*A personal, evolving question - what gives my life meaning?*)

The first question has been asked by philosophers, scientists, and spiritual thinkers for millennia. Some say life has no inherent purpose - it simply exists. Others believe life is a divine creation, part of a grand cosmic plan. But no answer is universally accepted, and perhaps no answer is needed.

The second question is more immediate. Even if life itself has no predetermined purpose, I still need a reason to wake up each morning. This is where my personal sense of purpose comes in - not as a fixed destiny, but as something I shape through my experiences, actions, and values.

Purpose as Evolution, Not a Fixed Destination

For a long time, I thought purpose was something I had to find - some singular mission I was meant to fulfil. But I now see that purpose is not something I am given; it is something I create. As a child, my purpose was to explore, to play, to learn. As a student, my purpose was to understand the world. As I grew older, my purpose shifted - to build a career, to form relationships, to contribute to something larger than myself. What I thought was my purpose five years ago may no longer be true today. And that is okay. Purpose is not a fixed destination; it is an evolving journey.

I have seen people redefine their purpose multiple times in life - a retired athlete becoming a mentor, a successful businessperson shifting to philanthropy, a scientist turning to art. If purpose were something fixed, then life would become meaningless the moment we achieved our initial goals. But if purpose is fluid, then life remains meaningful no matter what stage we are in.

Can Life Be Purposeful Even Without a Grand Mission?

Some people dedicate their lives to a specific cause or passion. Others do not feel drawn to any single, grand pursuit. Does that mean their lives lack purpose?

I once believed that purpose had to be extraordinary - that it had to be something that changed the world. But I have come to realize that purpose can be found in the smallest of actions like being present with loved ones, offering kindness to a stranger, creating something, no matter how small or even growing, learning, and experiencing life fully.

A tree does not question its purpose- it simply grows, provides shade, bears fruit, and eventually returns to the earth. Perhaps my purpose is no different- to live, to experience, to contribute in whatever way I can, and to let go when the time comes.

Living with Purpose, Without Attachment to It

Does having a purpose mean I must cling to it? No. I can be deeply committed to my purpose while also understanding that it may change. If I become too attached to a specific purpose, I may resist change when life pushes me in a new direction.

Purpose should serve as a guide, not a prison. It should give me direction but not limit my possibilities. If I hold onto one idea of purpose too rigidly, I may ignore the doors that open along the way.

The Bhagavad Gita speaks of "*Nishkama Karma*" - acting with purpose but without attachment to the results. I can dedicate myself to meaningful work, relationships, and self-growth without needing a specific outcome to validate my existence.

The Purpose of Life is to Live It Fully

I may never know the absolute purpose of life. But that does not mean life is meaningless. Meaning is not something I find - it is something I create, moment by moment. My purpose is not something I must chase - it is something I cultivate through how I live. It is not defined by success or failure - it is shaped by presence, engagement, and growth. It is not about eliminating suffering - it is about embracing the full spectrum of life.

Happiness comes and goes. Success rises and falls. But meaning remains - woven into the smallest of moments, in the choices I make, in the love I give, in the awareness with which I live.

I do not need a final answer to life's purpose. I only need
to live it.

Chapter 23

Motivations to Live – Why Do I Keep Going?

If life has no fixed, predetermined purpose, then why do I wake up every morning and engage with the world? Why do I chase dreams, build relationships, seek knowledge, and endure struggles? If I truly accept that everything is temporary, that all achievements will fade, and that life has no ultimate goal except the one I give it - then why does any of it matter?

There was a time when I wondered if knowing the truth about life's impermanence meant I should just let go of all effort, stop striving, and simply float along with whatever happened. If nothing is permanent, why build anything at all?

But I soon realized that letting go of illusions does not mean giving up on life. In fact, when I stopped attaching myself to fixed outcomes, I began to appreciate life more. I understood that the reason I live is not because I must fulfill some cosmic destiny, but because engaging with life is itself the experience I am here for.

But what exactly motivates me to keep going? What drives me, even when life is uncertain, even when struggles arise, even when there is no guarantee of happiness or success?

Survival and the Need for Security

At the most basic level, I am motivated to live because I must survive. My body seeks food, shelter, and safety. Life itself wants to continue. I do not need to create motivation for this - my biology takes care of it. No matter what I believe about life, my body still needs nourishment and rest. Even if money is not the ultimate goal, I need resources to live comfortably. If I do not take care of my body, my ability to experience life diminishes.

These basic needs may seem unimportant in a discussion on motivation, but without them, all higher motivations fade into irrelevance. A hungry, cold, and unsafe person does not reflect on existential questions - they focus on the next meal, the next shelter, the next moment of relief. These are the fundamental motivators that form the base of everything else.

The Drive for Growth and Achievement

Beyond survival, I am driven by the desire to grow. There is a natural urge within me to improve, to learn, to achieve something greater than where I started. This can be seen in everything - from the child who takes their first steps to the scientist pushing the boundaries of knowledge. Growth is intrinsic to life.

Mastery and progress bring a sense of fulfilment. Whether it is excelling in a career, building a skill, or learning something new, I feel alive when I grow. Challenges give me direction, providing a reason to move forward rather than stagnate. When I create something - a project, an idea, a piece of art - I feel connected to something larger than myself.

However, I have also learned that growth should not become an obsession. If I tie my identity solely to achievements, then every failure feels like a loss of self. I can grow without being attached to what I achieve. My motivation should not stem from fear of failure, but from the natural desire to expand my potential.

The Power of Relationships and Connection

If survival is about sustaining the body, and growth is about strengthening the mind, then connection is about nourishing the heart. I am not an isolated being. I live in a world filled with relationships - family, friends, mentors, colleagues, strangers. Even in solitude, I am shaped by the presence of others, whether physically or through their impact on my life.

Love and companionship add depth to my existence. Whether through family, friendships, or romantic love, relationships are a source of strength and learning. I do not just exist for myself - I exist in relation to others, and that makes life richer. Sometimes, my motivation is not just self-centred - it is also about giving, supporting, and being there for others.

Community and belonging create a sense of purpose. Even if I seek personal growth, I do not exist in isolation. Being part of something - a family, a group, a movement

- gives me a sense of meaning. But just as I should not tie my identity to achievement, I should also not tie it solely to relationships. Relationships bring meaning, but they do not define who I am.

The Desire to Explore and Understand

Beyond survival, beyond achievement, beyond relationships - there is another force that keeps me engaged with life: the desire to explore, to experience, to understand. Even if I had all my needs met, even if I had no external pressures, there would still be something within me that longs to **know.**

Curiosity drives me forward. I want to see the world from different perspectives, to understand what lies beyond my current awareness. The joy of discovery - whether through books, travel, conversations, or introspection - keeps me engaged. There is something thrilling about simply being part of it all.

This curiosity extends to deeper questions. Who am I beyond my identity? What is the nature of reality? These questions do not paralyze me; they inspire me to engage with life more deeply. The more I experience life without needing fixed answers, the more I see that the experience itself is enough.

How to Stay Motivated Without Being Trapped by Desire

One of the greatest challenges is how to stay engaged with life without becoming attached to external outcomes. If I chase achievement, I may burn out. If I cling to relationships, I may fear loss. If I define myself by a purpose, I may resist change.

I have learned to balance motivation with a sense of detachment - not as disinterest, but as freedom. I can pursue success without being defined by it. I can love deeply without fearing loss. I can seek growth without needing to prove anything.

Being present in the journey matters more than reaching a destination. Motivation does not have to be about accomplishing a final goal. The process of learning, experiencing, and growing is valuable in itself. What motivates me today may not be what drives me ten years from now. Allowing motivation to shift and evolve keeps life dynamic and open.

Living Fully, Without Needing a Grand Purpose

Do I need a grand reason to live? Perhaps not. But that does not mean life is meaningless. Meaning is not something I find - it is something I create, moment by moment.

I wake up because there is something to experience, something to learn, something to create. I keep going because there are people to love, things to understand, and places to explore. I engage with life not because I must, but because I can.

Some days, my motivation is big - I want to build something, achieve something, leave a mark. Other days, it is small - I want to enjoy a sunrise, have a meaningful conversation, or simply breathe deeply. Both are valid.

I do not need to justify my existence with an extraordinary mission. I do not need to find the one reason that makes life worth living. Life itself is the reason. And as long as I am here, I will live it fully.

Chapter 24

The Burden and Freedom of Choice

Every day, I make choices - some small, some life-changing. From what I eat to where I live, from my career decisions to the relationships I nurture, my life is shaped by the sum of my choices. It seems simple: I decide, I act, and I move forward. But the reality of choice is far more complex. At times, I have felt empowered by the choices before me, excited by the possibilities they offer. At other times, I have felt overwhelmed, afraid of making the wrong decision, paralyzed by uncertainty.

Choice is often spoken about as freedom, yet I have learned that choice is also a burden. The more options I have, the more responsibility I bear. Every decision I make rules out another, and every path I take is a path I leave behind. In a world that constantly tells me I can be anything, do anything, and have anything, I sometimes wonder: *What if I choose wrong? What if I regret my decision?*

At its core, the challenge of choice is not just about picking between options - it is about the weight I attach to my decisions. Am I choosing based on what I truly want, or am I choosing out of fear? Am I making decisions freely, or am I trapped by the expectations of society, family, or past conditioning?

The Anxiety of Infinite Possibilities

In an earlier time, choices were simpler. People followed the roles they were born into, their lives largely shaped by duty, tradition, and necessity. But today, I live in an age of infinite choices. I can choose where I live, what career to pursue, who to spend my life with, and how I define success. I can change directions at any moment, reinvent myself, and take a new path.

This should be liberating, yet sometimes, it feels suffocating. The modern world tells me I should make the *right* choices - ones that lead to success, happiness, and fulfilment. But how do I know which choice is the right one? If I make the wrong decision, will I be able to undo it? The more options I have, the greater my fear of choosing wrong.

I have often hesitated in making decisions, believing that a perfect choice exists - one that will bring me the ideal life, free from regret. But in seeking the perfect choice, I sometimes delay action, stuck in endless analysis, second-guessing myself. The irony is that in trying to make the best choice, I risk making no choice at all.

Regret: The Shadow of Choice

No matter how carefully I choose, I cannot escape the reality of regret. Every decision comes with trade-offs - paths I did not take, opportunities I let go of, possibilities I will never explore. Sometimes, I look back and wonder: *What if I had chosen differently? What if I had taken that other path?*

Regret is a powerful emotion, one that can consume me if I let it. But regret is also a teacher. It reminds me that choices are rarely perfect, that life is unpredictable, and that I cannot always foresee the consequences of my decisions. The key is to recognize that regret does not mean I failed - it means I lived, I took risks, and I learned.

Rather than fearing regret, I have learned to accept it as a natural part of life. Instead of dwelling on what I could have done differently, I focus on what I can do now. Every choice, even the ones that did not turn out as expected, has shaped me. The mistakes, the detours, the missteps - all of them have contributed to who I am.

Freedom in Accepting That No Choice is Final

One of the greatest misconceptions about choice is that it is permanent. I once believed that some decisions - career, relationships, life direction - were irreversible. But life is not static. Just as I change, so do my circumstances, my understanding, and my desires.

Many of the choices I once thought were life-defining have turned out to be just one step in a larger journey. I have taken paths that felt like dead ends, only to realize later that they led me to something unexpected. I have made decisions that seemed wrong at the time but eventually opened doors I never saw before.

This has taught me that choices are not prisons - they are starting points. If I make a decision and later realize it does not serve me, I can choose again. If I take a path and find that it no longer fulfils me, I can change directions. The real freedom of choice is not in making the perfect decision - it is in knowing that no decision is absolute.

Choosing for Myself vs. Choosing for Others

One of the hardest aspects of choice is separating what I truly want from what others expect of me. Many of my choices have been shaped by the desires of my family, society, or the fear of disappointing others. I have pursued opportunities that seemed prestigious rather than fulfilling, made decisions that aligned with expectations rather than my own desires.

But I have also seen what happens when people live their entire lives making choices for others. They achieve success but feel empty. They meet expectations but lose themselves in the process. A life built on external validation is fragile - one that can crumble the moment approval is withdrawn.

This does not mean I ignore my responsibilities or the people I care about. But it does mean I ask myself: *Am I choosing out of obligation or out of authenticity? Am I living a life that is truly mine, or one that was designed for me?*

When I start making choices that align with who I am rather than who I am supposed to be, I find true freedom.

The Balance Between Choice and Acceptance

There is a paradox to choice: while I strive to make decisions wisely, I also need to accept that I cannot control everything. I can choose my actions, but I cannot always choose their outcomes. I can make the best decision possible with the information I have, but life will unfold in ways I cannot predict.

This is where I find balance - not in obsessing over choices, but in making them with awareness and trust. If I spend my life trying to control every outcome, I will always live in fear. But if I choose with clarity and accept that uncertainty is a part of life, I can move forward with peace.

What This Means for My Life

I no longer see choices as burdens, but as invitations. Every decision I make is not about right or wrong - it is about growth, experience, and movement. I do not have to fear making mistakes, because mistakes are simply choices that lead to learning.

I embrace the freedom to choose, while also letting go of the illusion that I can always choose correctly. I understand that regret is inevitable, but it does not define me. I allow myself to change, to evolve, and to make new choices when necessary.

And most importantly, I remind myself that choice is not about finding the perfect path - it is about walking the path I choose with presence, courage, and awareness.

171

This Page has been intentionally left Blank

As the world shifts around me—digitally, culturally, globally— I begin to ask: Where do I end and the world begins? Do I shape my surroundings, or do they shape me? In this blur between the personal and the collective, the timeless 'I' navigates a world that is constantly in motion.

Section VI

The Expanding Self in a Changing World

Chapter 25

The Digital "I" – Am I More Than My Online Presence?

For most of human history, "I" existed only in the physical world. My identity was shaped by my interactions, relationships, and actions in the real world. But today, my existence extends beyond the physical - I have a digital self, a version of me that lives online, shaped by what I share, post, and consume.

At times, this digital presence feels empowering. It allows me to connect with people across the world, express myself in ways I never could before, and access knowledge instantly. But at other times, I wonder: *Is my digital self an extension of me, or has it become something separate? Am I shaping my online identity, or is it shaping me?*

I have found myself checking notifications compulsively, feeling validated by "likes" and "comments," and sometimes even questioning my worth based on how my online presence is perceived. The digital "I" has given me connection, but it has also brought new anxieties- *Do people see the real me? Am I curating my life rather than living it?*

Where do I end, and where does my digital-self begin?

The Digital Self: A Reflection or a Performance?

Social media and digital spaces give me a unique ability to craft my identity. I can choose what I share, how I present myself, and what aspects of my life I highlight. But this raises a question: *Is my digital self an authentic representation of me, or is it a performance?*

Studies in digital psychology suggest that most people present an idealized version of themselves online. Research by the American Psychological Association found that frequent social media users tend to compare their real lives with the curated lives of others, often leading to dissatisfaction and anxiety. This suggests that while I believe I am shaping my digital identity, I am also unconsciously shaping my self-perception in response to the polished, filtered realities I see online.

This was a realization I struggled with. I wanted to believe that my online self was just a reflection of me, but I began noticing subtle differences. The way I phrased things, the photos I chose, the moments I shared - none of these were lies, but they were curated. I was presenting not just who I was, but who I wanted to be seen as. Was I living for myself, or for an audience?

The Validation Loop: Seeking Meaning in Metrics

One of the most powerful aspects of digital life is instant feedback. In the real world, validation is slow - appreciation comes from relationships built over time. But online, a single post can bring immediate likes, shares, and comments, creating a sense of instant affirmation.

This has psychological consequences. Studies in neuroscience and social media show that receiving likes activates the dopamine reward system, the same system linked to pleasure from food, gambling, and even addiction. Over time, the brain begins associating social media engagement with self-worth, leading to a compulsive need for validation.

I have felt this pull myself - the small rush of excitement when a post gets attention, the slight disappointment when it doesn't. I started questioning: *Am I sharing because I want to, or because I need to be seen?*

The problem is not validation itself - humans are wired to seek connection and acknowledgment. The problem arises when external validation replaces internal validation, when my self-worth becomes dependent on digital approval. If I am constantly seeking affirmation online, who am I when no one is watching?

Am I the Consumer, or the Product?

One of the uncomfortable truths about the digital world is that I am not just a user - I am also the product. Every time I engage online, data is collected - my interests, my habits, my preferences. Algorithms track my behaviour, curating content designed to keep me engaged for as long as possible.

Tech companies use these insights to shape what I see, what I buy, and even what I think. Research on algorithmic influence shows that the more time I spend online, the more the digital world moulds my beliefs and behaviours, often without my awareness.

This realization was unsettling. I had always believed that I was in control of my digital presence, but I began to see how my online world was being shaped for me. The posts I engaged with influenced what I saw next. The news I read was tailored to reinforce my existing beliefs. My choices were subtly nudged in directions I never consciously chose.

In a world where the digital "I" is constantly being influenced, how do I remain truly authentic?

Escaping the Digital Self Without Disconnecting

There were times I considered stepping away from the digital world altogether. I imagined deleting social media, disengaging from online spaces, and returning to a world free from notifications and curated identities. But I knew this was neither realistic nor necessary.

The digital world is not inherently harmful - it is a tool. Like any tool, it depends on how I use it. Instead of disconnecting, I had to learn to engage with awareness.

Reclaiming My Digital Presence

Instead of mindlessly scrolling, I started asking: *Why am I here?* If I was using social media for learning, connection, or inspiration, it was valuable. But if I was using it to escape, compare, or seek validation, I stepped back.

I became more conscious of how algorithms shaped my online world. I diversified my sources of information, questioned my own biases, and made an effort to consume content actively rather than passively.

Studies show that digital interactions do not provide the same depth of emotional fulfilment as real-world connections. I began prioritizing face-to-face conversations, shared experiences, and personal moments that did not need an audience.

I reminded myself that my value is not measured in likes, comments, or followers. My worth is not tied to how my digital self is perceived, but to how I experience life beyond the screen.

What This Means for My Life

I no longer see my digital self as **separate from me**, but I also no longer allow it to define me. It is an extension - a tool for expression, connection, and learning. But **it is not my identity**.

I no longer seek validation through screens. I engage online, but I do not let it consume my reality. I share my thoughts, but I do not shape them based on how they will be received. I use the digital world with **intention**, but I no longer let it shape my self-worth.

In the end, **I am more than my online presence**. The digital "I" is just one reflection of me, but the real "I" exists beyond the screen - in the moments no one captures, in the thoughts I do not post, and in the life I live, fully present, whether or not anyone is watching.

Chapter 26

The World and Me – How Much Should I Engage?

From the moment I wake up, the world calls for my attention. News headlines flash updates about global crises, social movements demand action, and the voices of millions compete for space in the digital and physical spheres. I am constantly reminded that I am not just an individual - I am part of something bigger.

Yet, I find myself caught between two opposing forces. On one hand, I feel the urge to engage, to contribute, to care. On the other, I feel overwhelmed by the weight of it all. How much of the world's suffering should I take on? Where is the balance between being informed and being consumed? If I withdraw completely, am I being selfish? If I engage fully, will I lose myself?

The question is no longer just about what is happening in the world - it is about how much of it should become part of me.

The Paradox of Awareness: Knowing More, Feeling Less?

With technology and constant connectivity, I know more about the world than any generation before me. A hundred years ago, people were primarily concerned with their immediate surroundings. Today, in a matter of minutes, I can learn about an earthquake across the globe, political conflicts in distant countries, economic crises affecting millions. I can hear thousands of opinions on what I should care about, how I should feel, and what I should do.

But something strange has happened. The more I am exposed to, the more helpless I sometimes feel. Psychological studies refer to this as "compassion fatigue" - a phenomenon where, after prolonged exposure to global crises, people start feeling emotionally numb rather than empathetic. My mind, unable to process endless suffering, begins to shut down its emotional response.

I have seen this in myself. There was a time when every tragic news story hit me deeply. But after a while, I noticed a shift - not because I stopped caring, but because my ability to process it all had limits. Knowing about the world's problems did not always give me the power to fix them; sometimes, it just left me feeling powerless.

Does this mean I should disengage? Ignore what is happening? Pretend the world's problems are not mine?

The Illusion of Individual Responsibility for the World

One of the biggest struggles I have faced is the feeling that if I care about something, I must do something about it. The burden of responsibility can be overwhelming - should I fight against inequality, advocate for climate action, donate to every cause that needs help? The more I learn, the more I realize how much needs to be done. But is it realistic for one person to carry the weight of the entire world?

Philosophers have long debated the moral obligation of individuals toward society. Utilitarian thinkers like John Stuart Mill argue that we should act in ways that maximize happiness for the greatest number of people. But existentialist philosophers like Jean-Paul Sartre caution against losing oneself in grand causes - meaning must be chosen, not imposed.

For me, this has been a difficult balance to strike. I want to be responsible, but I also do not want to dissolve my own identity into causes that may or may not align with what truly matters to me.

I have begun to see that I cannot be responsible for everything, but I can be responsible for something. Instead of being paralyzed by all the world's problems, I can choose where I focus my energy.

Engagement Without Losing Myself

I have learned that the key to engaging with the world without being consumed by it is intentionality. It is about choosing how, where, and when I engage, rather than reacting to every crisis, every opinion, every demand for attention.

I do not need to act on everything I know. There is value in awareness itself - understanding the world, being informed, and thinking critically. But action should come from a place of clarity, not obligation. If I try to fix everything, I will fix nothing.

The world is vast, but my immediate surroundings are where my impact is strongest. If I want to contribute, I must ask: *Where can I actually make a difference?* Instead of feeling responsible for every issue, I focus on what I can influence - my community, my work, my relationships.

Engaging with the world does not mean losing myself in it. I have learned to take breaks from the noise, to step back from media consumption, and to remind myself that it is okay to care without being consumed. Even the most dedicated activists take time to rest.

I once believed that if I was not constantly engaged in improving the world, I was being selfish. But the truth is, burnout does not help anyone. I remind myself that it is not my job to fix everything - it is enough to do my part.

The Risk of Over-Engagement: When the World Takes Over "I"

There was a time when I felt guilty for prioritizing my personal happiness while knowing that suffering existed in the world. But I realized that there is no contradiction between engaging with the world and taking care of myself.

In Buddhism, the concept of "right action" teaches that compassion must be balanced with wisdom. A drowning person cannot save others. A person exhausted by outrage cannot meaningfully contribute to change. Engagement must be sustainable - otherwise, it leads to cynicism and withdrawal.

I have met people who became so immersed in activism, politics, or social issues that they lost their own joy. Every conversation became about injustice, every action about fighting against something. While their passion was admirable, many eventually burned out - not because they did not care, but because they forgot to live outside of their cause.

This made me ask myself: *If my engagement with the world makes me constantly anxious, bitter, or exhausted, is it truly serving its purpose?*

What This Means for My Life

I no longer see the world as something I must either fully embrace or completely shut out. I have realized that I can be informed without being overwhelmed, engaged without being consumed, compassionate without being exhausted.

I no longer feel guilty for focusing on my own growth, my own happiness, my own inner world. I engage where I can, I help where I am able, and I trust that I am part of a much larger collective effort.

The world does not need me to fix everything. It needs people who are grounded, clear-minded, and willing to contribute in ways that are sustainable. And that is what I choose to be.

I am a part of the world - but I am also my own person. And I no longer believe those two things must be in conflict.

Chapter 27

Culture and Tradition – Evolving or Trapped?

For much of my life, I have existed within the framework of culture and tradition, absorbing them without questioning. They have given me a sense of belonging, shaped my understanding of right and wrong, and influenced how I interact with the world. Yet, as I have grown, I have begun to wonder - do these inherited structures truly define who I am, or do they merely shape how I perceive myself?

Culture and tradition are not just external forces; they are deeply embedded in my identity. The language I speak, the rituals I observe, the values I hold - all are products of the environment I was born into. But if these external elements have moulded me, then how much of "I" is truly independent? And if I question them, am I betraying my roots or merely seeking my own truth?

Culture: A Lens or a Limitation?

Culture is more than just a set of customs or traditions - it is the lens through which I have been conditioned to interpret the world. It dictates what is considered normal, acceptable, and even desirable. Yet, the more I examine culture, the more I realize that its influence extends far beyond visible rituals.

There are quite a few instances. The words I use not only help me communicate but also shape how I think. Different cultures have unique ways of expressing emotions and abstract concepts, which means my very perception of reality has been framed by the language I speak.

In some cultures, success is measured by financial status and material accumulation. In others, it is defined by knowledge, social harmony, or spiritual attainment. The values I chase in life are largely determined by the cultural framework I was born into.

My sense of right and wrong is deeply influenced by cultural upbringing. What one society considers a virtue; another may see as a flaw. My ethical instincts may not always stem from universal truth but from learned behaviour

The roles assigned to men and women vary across cultures. Some societies encourage rigid gender roles, while others are more fluid in their definitions. The expectations placed upon me regarding my ambitions, responsibilities, and even emotions have been shaped by these cultural norms.

If my thoughts, desires, and moral values are shaped by culture, then how much of my identity is truly mine? Where does the influence of my environment end, and where does the true "I" begin?

Tradition: A Source of Strength or a Burden?

Tradition provides continuity - a thread connecting generations. It carries the wisdom of the past, offering stability in an ever-changing world. Many traditions give life meaning, whether through festivals that bring communities together, rituals that encourage mindfulness, or values that promote ethical living.

However, tradition can also be limiting. It can impose outdated ideas, resist progress, and create obligations that no longer serve their original purpose. When a tradition is followed without understanding, it ceases to be a guide and becomes a rule. I have often asked myself - am I honouring tradition, or am I trapped by it?

Some traditions evolve naturally, adapting to the needs of the present. Others resist change, holding on to outdated norms long after they have lost relevance.

Many cultures once maintained rigid social hierarchies. Over time, some of these structures have loosened, yet in many places, they persist, restricting opportunity and reinforcing inequality.

Traditional expectations often dictated that men be providers and women be caretakers. Today, these roles are shifting, allowing for greater personal freedom. But resistance to change still exists, leading to a struggle between personal aspirations and societal expectations.

Many rituals were created in response to historical or environmental needs, but over time, their original purpose has been lost. Some continue to be followed out of habit rather than conscious choice.

This leads to an important question: Should tradition be preserved simply because it has always been followed? Or should it be examined, refined, and adapted?

The Evolution of Culture: Resistance vs. Renewal

A common argument against change is that altering traditions will dilute cultural identity. Many fear that modernization leads to homogenization, erasing the uniqueness of different societies. Languages disappear, folk traditions fade, and indigenous knowledge systems struggle to survive in a globalized world.

Yet, culture has never been static. What is considered "traditional" today was once a break from the past. Many of the things I see as cultural norms were shaped by historical events, migrations, and societal shifts.

Centuries ago, arranged marriages were the norm in many societies. Today, love marriages, inter-caste unions, and even independent choices about marriage are becoming more accepted.

The way people speak today is vastly different from how they did centuries ago. Languages borrow from one another, adapt to new realities, and reflect the changing needs of communication.

Traditional diets were shaped by geography and necessity. Today, food choices are influenced by ethics, health consciousness, and global influences.

These changes do not necessarily mean cultural decay. Rather, they show that culture is alive, responding to the realities of the time. A culture that refuses to evolve becomes stagnant. A culture that adapts remains relevant.

How Do I Engage with Culture Consciously?

If I blindly follow traditions, I risk losing my ability to think for myself. If I reject them outright, I risk losing the richness they offer. The key is to engage with culture consciously - to participate in it with awareness, rather than out of obligation.

To do this, I ask myself: *Does this cultural belief or practice help me grow, or does it restrict me? Am I following this tradition because it aligns with my values, or because I fear judgment? Can I respect culture without being bound by it?*

When I approach culture with awareness, I do not feel the need to accept or reject it completely. I can retain what resonates with me and discard what does not. I can celebrate traditions that bring joy and meaning while questioning those that enforce limitations.

Culture and the Infinite "I"

If I am truly infinite - beyond labels, roles, and external definitions - then where does culture fit into my understanding of self?

Culture is an experience, not an identity. It is something I participate in, not something that defines me. The realization of the infinite "I" is not about rejecting culture but about understanding its place. Culture offers context, not confinement.

With this perspective I am free to honor my cultural heritage without being bound by it. I can evolve beyond inherited identities without losing my connection to the past. I can engage with tradition while remaining open to personal and collective growth.

What This Means for My Life

I no longer see culture as something fixed that I must either protect or reject. Instead, I see it as a conversation between past, present, and future. Some traditions ground me, offering meaning and continuity. Others no longer serve me, and I am free to move beyond them.

By questioning what I inherit, embracing what is valuable, and letting go of what confines me, I do not lose my identity - I reclaim it. Culture does not define me; it is one of many experiences that shape my journey. And when I engage with it consciously, I do not feel trapped by tradition - I feel empowered to shape it.

Having wandered through the world and the self, you now arrive at the edge of deeper truths. What is real? What is illusion? What lies beyond fear, time, and identity? As you enter this final stretch, let go of the search for answers. Let what remains reveal itself.

Section VII

Self-Realization and Liberation

Chapter 28

The Search for Meaning – Do I Need Religion?

As a child, I was introduced to religion before I could fully grasp its meaning. I learned to bow, to pray, to listen to stories of gods, sages, miracles, and morals. Religion gave shape to the unknown - it made sense of fear, joy, death, and the invisible. It was the language in which I first met the idea of something larger than myself.

But as I grew older, I began to question: Is religion a doorway to truth - or a wall that confines it? Does it connect me to the divine - or distance me from myself? Must I believe in a specific form of God to find meaning - or can meaning be found beyond form?

These questions didn't signal the end of faith. Rather, they marked the beginning of a deeper journey - one that led me from external religion to internal realization.

Beyond Belief: What Are We Really Seeking?

Across cultures and centuries, every religion has asked the same questions: Who am I? Why am I here? What lies beyond death? And what is the nature of this vast, mysterious existence?

Whether it's the Vedas of India, the teachings of Christ in the New Testament, the Sufi poetry of Rumi, or the reflections of Zen masters, religion has always pointed inward - toward the mystery and miracle of human consciousness itself.

When Christ said, *"The kingdom of God is within you"* (Luke 17:21), he was not prescribing a belief system. He was revealing that divinity is not far away, but already present. When the Chandogya Upanishad proclaimed, *"Tat Tvam Asi"*- "That Thou Art" - it pointed not to a god above the clouds, but to the divine self within me.

Religious belief, in this light, becomes secondary. The primary goal is direct experience - of truth, peace, and unity. Whether I walk through a temple, church, mosque, or forest, the question is the same: Do I know who I truly am?

Advaita Vedanta: No Separation, No Division

Among all the systems of religious and philosophical thought I explored, it was Advaita Vedanta that offered the clearest lens through which to see the infinite nature of "I." Advaita means "non-dual." It teaches that there is no real separation between the self (Atman) and the absolute reality (Brahman). They are one and the same.

This realization is not theoretical. It is the end of the search.

The Mandukya Upanishad says, *"Ayam Atma Brahma"* - *"This Self is Brahman."* The divine is not out there, but right here, as the very awareness in which my thoughts, feelings, and experiences arise.

In this sense, religion is not about pleasing a God outside me, but about recognizing the godhood within - not in an egoic way, but in a deeply humbling way. The moment I understand that the consciousness within me is not separate from the source of all creation, I no longer feel alone, insecure, or incomplete.

Stories That Point to Inner Awakening

Across traditions, there are stories that, when read deeply, hint at this same truth.

When Ramana Maharshi was asked, "Should I believe in God?" he replied, *"First find out who is asking the question."* His path was simple: self-inquiry. He did not reject religion, but redirected it inward - toward the question, "Who am I?"

In the Bhagavad Gita, Krishna says to Arjuna, *"I am the Self, seated in the heart of all beings."* Here too, the divine is not outside, but within each living being. Arjuna's battlefield is symbolic of the inner war each of us faces - between ego and truth, illusion and clarity.

Even in Sufi mysticism, the poetry of Rumi sings of union with the Divine Beloved - not through ritual, but through the annihilation of the self. *"You are not a drop in the ocean. You are the entire ocean in a drop,"* he wrote, echoing the very spirit of Advaita.

These are not just poetic ideas. They are radical shifts in how I see myself and reality.

The Trap of Externalization

Yet, in many places, religion has become external-focused on rites, obedience, identity, and tribal boundaries. Instead of leading me to unity, it often reinforces division: between believer and non-believer, saved and damned, pure and impure.

At its worst, religion becomes a source of fear - fear of sin, fear of judgment, fear of divine punishment. I have seen people follow rituals out of compulsion rather than joy. I have prayed not from love, but from anxiety.

But fear cannot reveal the infinite. It only binds the mind in illusion. True awakening comes not when I fear God, but when I realize that nothing separates me from the divine.

The Buddha never claimed divinity - he asked us to inquire. Jesus invited us to live with love, not to memorize commandments. The essence of every religion lies not in dogma, but in transformation.

Rituals: Means, Not the End

I still light a lamp. I still chant. I still visit temples and sacred spaces. But I do so with awareness. These are not obligations. They are tools - reminders of the sacred.

A ritual done with awareness becomes meditation. A prayer uttered with presence becomes communion. But when rituals become empty repetition, they no longer serve.

The Bhagavad Gita warns against mechanical action: *"Even the wise act with awareness. Without awareness, even right actions bind."*

So, I ask myself: Does this ritual open my heart, or shut it? Does it bring clarity, or more noise? The outer must serve the inner - not the other way around.

Spirituality Without Religion?

Some find meaning outside organized religion. They meditate, reflect, and walk their own path. They are not "unbelievers" - they are seekers. In fact, some of the most spiritually awake people I know have no religious label.

But labels do not matter. Only depth does.

Whether I call myself religious, spiritual, or neither, the real question is: Am I willing to know the truth of what I am? If the answer is yes, then I am already on the path - whatever name it takes.

What This Means for My Life

I no longer see religion as a structure I must fit into. I see it as a path I can walk with awareness. If it helps me dissolve the ego, I embrace it. If it strengthens the ego, I let it go.

I respect all paths, but I follow none blindly. I see God not in images, but in awareness. I do not reject rituals, but I refuse to be ruled by them. I still listen to chants, read scriptures, and bow in reverence - but I know that the real temple is the self.

Religion may help open the door, but what lies beyond is not something that can be named, taught, or worshipped - it must be realized. And that realization is not religious - it is truth itself.

Chapter 29

What Is Real? What Is Illusion?

For much of my life, I assumed reality was self-evident. What I see, touch, hear, and feel must be real. The people I know, the thoughts I have, the world I move through - all of this seemed beyond question.

And yet, the more I have reflected on what this book is truly about - *the nature of "I"* - the more I have been forced to confront an uncomfortable possibility: Could it be that what I experience as real is not reality itself, but only a version shaped by my mind?

This question is not academic. It is the foundation of self-awareness. If what I see is not necessarily what is, then who am I in all this? What can I truly trust?

Perception and the Mind's Interpretation

Modern neuroscience offers a startling insight: the brain constructs reality. My senses pick up signals, but my mind assembles them into a coherent world. I don't see things as they are - I see them as my brain interprets them.

Take optical illusions. Or the experience of dreaming - where an entire world can be fabricated in sleep, complete with people, emotions, and consequences, only to disappear upon waking. In those moments, I believe the illusion completely.

Even in waking life, my attention is selective, my interpretation biased, and my memory unreliable. This tells me that my version of reality is a mental model, not a mirror of the world.

What Philosophy Has Always Warned Me

Long before neuroscience, philosophy questioned reality. In *Plato's Cave*, people mistake shadows for truth. In *Descartes' Meditations*, the thinker doubts everything except the fact that he is thinking.

But it is in the Upanishads and Advaita Vedanta that I find the clearest voice:

"The world is not unreal. But it is not ultimately real either. It is *Maya* - a dependent appearance, arising in consciousness."

Reality, they say, is not the transient form, but the unmoving awareness that observes all forms. What I call the world is like waves on the ocean - temporary, changing, and illusory unless I remember the water beneath.

The Illusions Within My Mind

Even if I accept the illusion in the outer world, there is another layer - the illusion within. How often have I suffered not because of what happened, but because of what I thought about it?

My mind tells stories. It assumes, predicts, exaggerates, fears, craves. And I believe it. I create imaginary futures, replay painful pasts, build identities around fleeting feelings. And in doing so, I lose touch with the quiet presence behind it all.

This presence - the one that watches even the doubting mind - is untouched by illusion. It is the only thing I know to be real.

The Greatest Illusion: The Self

Perhaps the deepest illusion is the belief in a separate, permanent self. Neuroscience cannot find it. Buddhism denies its independent existence. Vedanta calls it a false identification.

What I call "I" is a bundle of memories, thoughts, and roles. These change constantly. Yet something watches. Something *is* - regardless of what thought arises. That *something* is not a role, a belief, or a personality. It is awareness itself.

What This Means for My Life

I no longer chase certainty in the external world. I no longer cling to a fixed identity. I live in a world of appearances - but I am not bound by them. I may still act, love, fail, succeed, and grieve. But I do not confuse any of it for the unchanging truth of who I am. I am not the illusion - I am that in which the illusion appears.

In seeing what is not real, I come closer to that which *is*.
And in that quiet recognition, the question ends - not with an answer, but with stillness.

Chapter 30

Breaking Free – Living Without Fear

For much of my life, fear has lived alongside me - not as a dramatic intruder, but as a quiet, persistent voice. It whispers before every decision, questions every risk, and holds me back just when I'm about to move forward. Sometimes it poses as caution. Sometimes it dresses up as logic. But beneath it all is the same energy: the fear of what might go wrong.

Not all fear is irrational. There is a kind of fear that protects. But more often, fear becomes a habitual response - not to danger, but to discomfort, change, uncertainty, and vulnerability. It creeps in when I consider speaking my truth, changing direction, or stepping into the unknown. It tells me stories of what could go wrong. It magnifies failure, embarrassment, and rejection. It shrinks possibility down to safety.

I began to wonder: What would life look like if fear didn't control me? How much have I not lived - not because something was impossible, but because I was afraid?

Fear: A Habit of the Conditioned Mind

Fear is ancient. It is hardwired into the human brain as a survival tool. Our ancestors needed fear to avoid predators, survive hunger, and respond to danger. But today, those physical threats have largely faded - and yet, the brain continues to respond as if every uncertainty is a matter of life or death.

Modern fear is not usually about survival. It is psychological - imagined futures, social expectations, loss of image, or deviation from the familiar. Neuroscience shows that the same brain circuits activate whether I am facing an actual threat or merely thinking about one. In other words, most of my fear is not about what is happening now - it is about what *might* happen later.

This means my fear is not reality - it is a story. It is a mental simulation, a forecast based on past conditioning. And if fear is a story, then I am not obligated to believe it. I can examine it, question it, and choose not to be controlled by it.

The Faces Fear Wears

Fear does not always announce itself. It hides under masks - disguised as responsibility, humility, reason, or even morality. I had to learn to recognize its many forms like the fear of failure made me seek only what I was already good at, the fear of rejection silenced me in moments I wanted to speak, the fear of uncertainty kept me in situations I had long outgrown, the fear of loss made me cling to people, possessions, and ideas that no longer served me or the fear of insignificance led me to overperform, to prove I mattered.

Each of these fears seemed unique, but they all pointed to the same root: identification with a fragile, limited self-image- the "I" that is constantly measuring, comparing, protecting, defending.

Avoidance Is Not Freedom

For a long time, I believed that by avoiding what I feared, I was being wise. But I was not free - I was trapped. Every time I avoided a difficult conversation, every time I walked away from discomfort, every time I played small to stay safe, I was feeding the fear. I wasn't escaping it - I was reinforcing it.

I realized that fear feeds on avoidance. The only way to weaken it was to face it - not recklessly, but deliberately. To observe it, understand it, and gently walk through it.

And in doing so, I discovered something unexpected: most fears dissolved the moment I moved toward them. What I thought was a wall was often a shadow. The fear of doing something was greater than doing it.

The Shift: From Fear to Awareness

Courage, I came to understand, is not the absence of fear. It is the willingness to act despite it. But true fearlessness goes even deeper - it arises not from bravery, but from insight. From the realization that fear is a product of identification with the finite, conditioned self.

Fear only binds me when I believe I am the ego - the bundle of stories, memories, roles, and expectations. That self is always under threat - of failure, of irrelevance, of death. But when I rest in the awareness behind all these identities, I find something untouched by fear.

That awareness - the Infinite "I" - does not fear the fall because it was never trying to climb. It does not fear loss because it does not own. It does not fear change because it does not cling. It witnesses everything, but it is bound by nothing.

Reclaiming My Life from Fear

Breaking free from fear was not a one-time act. It became a practice - of choosing truth over illusion, action over paralysis, and presence over anxiety. It meant asking: am I acting out of fear or from clarity, is this decision driven by love or by avoidance or am I protecting an identity, or responding from awareness?

It also meant learning to sit with discomfort - to feel fear without running from it. Each time I stayed present with fear and didn't obey it, its grip loosened. It was not easy. But it was liberating.

What This Means for My Life

I no longer try to eliminate fear. That would be fighting shadows. Instead, I let it come, and I see it for what it is - thoughts, sensations, memories. I listen, and then I choose.

Fear may still visit. But it no longer decides. And as I let go of fear, I find space - space to speak, to move, to create, to love. I begin to live not from protection, but from truth.

The journey is not about becoming fearless. It is about discovering the part of me that was never afraid to begin with - the silent, spacious awareness that holds all experience, but is not defined by any of it.

That is the Infinite "I." And that "I" was never in chains.

Chapter 31

The Inevitable Passage – Aging, Mortality, and the End of the Body

For much of my life, I have taken my body for granted. In my youth, I believed it was limitless - I could push it, exhaust it, and it would still recover. I rarely stopped to think about aging, about how this very body that carried me through life would one day begin to slow down, weaken, and ultimately fail.

Aging is something I once observed in others, something that seemed distant and disconnected from me. I saw the elderly struggling to walk, their hands trembling, their backs hunched. I noticed how their voices softened, how their energy faded, how they spoke of memories as though they were treasures from another world. But I did not truly understand aging until I began to feel it myself.

It starts subtly - small aches that take longer to go away, a stiffness in the joints that was not there before, a decline in stamina, in eyesight, in reflexes. There comes a moment when I realize that no matter how well I take care of myself, the body has its own timeline, its own journey, independent of my desires.

We spend years strengthening our bodies, feeding them, clothing them, maintaining them - yet, eventually, no amount of care can stop the inevitable process of decay. The body is not permanent. It was never meant to be.

The Loss of Control Over One's Own Being

As the body weakens, I begin to lose the autonomy I once had. I may need help with things that once felt effortless - climbing stairs, carrying bags, even standing for too long. The hands that were once steady begin to shake. The legs that carried me miles now hesitate. The eyes that once saw the world clearly now blur its edges.

There is an emotional weight to this deterioration - not just in the pain of physical decline, but in the loss of independence. To rely on others for basic needs, to have to ask for help, to feel that I am no longer as capable as I once was - this is a kind of suffering few talk about. The mind may remain sharp, but the body begins to disobey. And one day, even the mind follows.

I have seen people who were once powerful, intelligent, and capable reduced to frail versions of their former selves. Their voices lose their authority. Their decisions are second-guessed. They are treated as though they have faded, as though they are no longer fully present in the world they helped build. The world moves forward, and they become invisible.

Watching Loved Ones Fade – A Mirror to My Own Mortality

Perhaps one of the most painful aspects of aging is not just experiencing it myself but witnessing it in those I love. I have seen parents grow weaker, their once strong hands now delicate, their voices carrying the weight of years. I have seen friends who were once full of life slowly withdraw, their bodies betraying them.

I have sat beside hospital beds, watching someone I love, take their final breaths, knowing that I, too, will one day lie in that bed. I have seen eyes that were once filled with recognition become distant, memories erased by time. I have heard the silence of a room that once held laughter, and I have felt the unbearable truth that everything - every person, every relationship, every experience - will one day be gone.

There is no escaping this reality. No one is exempt. No amount of wealth, power, or knowledge can prevent the certainty of decline and death.

The Fear of Death – And the Surrender to It

For much of my life, I feared death - not just my own, but the death of those I loved. The idea of ceasing to exist, of disappearing into nothingness, of losing all that I have known was overwhelming. I wondered: Will I be ready when the time comes? Will I fight against it, or will I accept it?

There comes a point when resistance becomes futile. The body will give in. The mind will slow. The senses will fade. And in that moment, I will have no choice but to surrender.

Yet, death is not an enemy. It is not something unnatural. It is, in fact, the most natural thing of all. Everything that is born must die. Every tree, every animal, every living being follows this path. The seasons change, the tides rise and fall, and so do we.

I have seen those who resist death until their final breath, clinging to life with fear. And I have seen those who meet it with peace, as though they have made their peace with impermanence. What makes the difference? What allows one person to let go while another fights until the end?

Perhaps the key is understanding that life was never ours to hold onto in the first place.

The Gentle Release – When the 'I' Begins to Dissolve

As the body deteriorates, as the senses grow dull, something else happens - the self, the "I" I have identified with my whole life, begins to fade. The things that once mattered - my achievements, my possessions, my reputation - start to feel distant, as though they belonged to another version of me.

I have seen elders who, in their final days, let go of everything. They no longer worry about ambitions, about unfinished tasks, about the past or the future. They simply exist in the moment, watching, breathing, being. The things that once defined them no longer hold weight. They are just… there.

And when the final moment arrives, when the breath slows, when the body takes its last sigh, what remains?

The world moves on. People grieve, then they continue their lives. Everything I built, everything I held onto, everything I once thought was so important - will dissolve, as though it never existed.

And yet, there is a strange peace in this. The realization that I was never separate from life itself. That the body was always meant to return to the earth, and that life continues, just as it always has.

Death is Not the End - It is a Continuation

If life is a journey, then death is simply another step forward. It is not an end, but a transition. Just as a wave rises and falls back into the ocean, so too does life return to where it came from.

I no longer see death as a tragedy, but as a part of existence itself. Just as I once entered this world, one day I will leave it. And in that final moment, when everything fades, I will not be afraid.

Because just as I let go of my childhood, my youth, my strength, and my past - one day, I will let go of life itself.

And perhaps, in that letting go, I will finally understand what it means to truly be free.

Chapter 32

Living Fully in the Present

For most of my life, I have moved through time like a traveller passing through a series of imagined destinations. I have lived waiting for the future - waiting to succeed, to be loved, to find peace. I have also looked back often - reliving joys, regretting mistakes, carrying the weight of memory. In this passage through time, one thing remained constant: I was almost never fully here.

I believed that my mind's ability to remember and anticipate was what made me human. But I began to see something deeper - this very ability also kept me in chains. While I was busy planning, comparing, and reminiscing, life was unfolding right now, and I was missing it. My mind lived in time, but my true self-awareness itself - existed only in the now.

Time is not the enemy. But my identification with the story of time - my past, my future, my becoming - prevented me from seeing the timeless presence that I truly am.

Why the Present Is So Elusive

The present moment is the only place where life happens, and yet it is the hardest place to stay. Why?

Because the mind is conditioned to move. It drifts between what was and what could be. It wants control over outcomes and clarity about the future. It clings to identity, which is built from memory and sustained by projection.

This tendency is not wrong - it is natural. Evolutionarily, it helped us survive. But now, it often serves not survival, but anxiety. My thoughts about the past become regret. My thoughts about the future become fear. And my thoughts about the present are often lost in judgment, comparison, or distraction.

I began to see that the difficulty in living in the present does not lie in the present itself - it lies in the mind's refusal to be still.

The Mind, Time, and the Illusion of "I"

When I say, "I was thinking," "I am worried," or "I will succeed," I reinforce the idea that I am a person moving through time. But who is this "I" that moves?

Am I really a timeline of events - a body aging, a mind developing, a person growing? Or am I the constant awareness in which all these movements appear?

The more I observed my thoughts, the more I realized that time lives only in the mind. My body exists now. The sky exists now. Experience always happens now. It is only the mind that divides reality into before, now, and later. And when I believe those divisions, I forget who I am.

The past and the future are not places - they are thoughts. And the thinker of those thoughts- the one who witnesses memory and imagination - is always here, always still, always now.

The Practice of Presence

Living in the present is not a technique; it is a shift in identity. It is recognizing that I am not the thinker - I am the awareness in which thoughts rise and fall.

But awareness is subtle, and the pull of mind is strong. So, I began gently training myself to return - to the breath, to sensation, to sound, to stillness. Not because the present is better, but because it is real.

Here are the practices that helped me reconnect: I stopped doing many things at once. If I am drinking tea, I drink tea. If I am walking, I walk. If I am with someone, I listen - not just with ears, but with presence. My body is always now. By focusing on sound, light, touch, or breath, I come home to the present effortlessly. I stopped fighting the mind. I let it wander, but I watched it - like clouds drifting across a still sky. In watching, I remembered that I am not my thoughts. I began welcoming silence - not as absence, but as presence. I allowed pauses between activity, not to achieve something, but to simply be. Everything I love, everything I fear, everything I am - is passing. And yet, something in me remains unchanged. When I embrace the fleeting nature of life, I stop resisting it and begin living it.

The Freedom of Now

Freedom does not come from having no past or knowing the future. It comes from seeing that the past is memory, the future is imagination, and the only truth is this moment - ever fresh, ever new.

This moment is enough. It holds no judgment, no identity, no story - only pure being. And in this space, I see that the Infinite "I" is not something I have to become. It is something I already am, whenever I stop searching and start noticing.

In the now, there is no fear - because fear lives in the future. In the now, there is no regret - because regret belongs to the past. In the now, there is no separate "I" - only life unfolding, watched silently by awareness.

What This Means for My Life

I no longer chase moments, because I know that this one is all there ever is. I no longer escape into memory or projection, because I see their unreality. I do not reject the mind, but I no longer let it lead. I walk with it, aware of the presence behind it.

The present is not a doorway to the Infinite "I." It *is* the Infinite "I." It is where all illusion ends, and reality begins - not as a concept, but as a living experience.

To live in the present is not a spiritual technique - it is the return to what I already am. And in that return, there is peace.

Chapter 33

The Universe and Me – A Mirror of the Infinite

There are moments when I step outside at night, look up at the stars, and feel something stir deep within me. It's not fear. It's not even curiosity. It's a kind of quiet awe - a pause in my thoughts as I realize how vast the universe is, and how tiny I am in comparison.

Billions of galaxies, each with billions of stars. As of what we currently observe, the universe contains more than 2 trillion galaxies, and that's only what our instruments can detect. The observable universe stretches over 93 billion light-years, and beyond that, we know nothing for certain. Time, space, light, energy - all swirling in patterns far beyond my grasp.

And here I am - one person, on one planet, orbiting one star, in one galaxy among trillions. What is the weight of my worries in all this? My regrets? My fears? My ambitions? They seem to disappear into silence, like a whisper against a roaring sea.

A Moment of Cosmic Humility

This realization does something to me. It humbles me.

The life I have taken so seriously - every success, every insult, every expectation - suddenly feels fragile. I have spent years trying to define who I am. I have clung to stories, to names, to roles. But in the face of this cosmic scale, do any of those truly matter?

The galaxies do not care if I am praised or ignored. The stars are not dimmed by my sadness. The black holes do not wait for me to figure out my purpose. The universe simply is - expanding, moving, existing - without the slightest awareness of "me."

And yet, I *am* aware of it.

I am here, on this small patch of Earth, gazing at something infinitely vast, trying to understand it. And in that moment, the question arises: What is it within me that is capable of perceiving the infinite?

The Paradox of Insignificance and Awareness

Science tells me I am made of the same elements that formed the stars - carbon, oxygen, nitrogen, hydrogen. My body, my brain, even my thoughts are born of atoms that have travelled across cosmic distances and epochs.

So yes, I am small. But perhaps, I am not insignificant. Because something within me is able to ask: *What is this universe? What am I doing here? What is this experience of being alive?* If I were only an organism among billions, how could I be capable of such wonder?

There is a strange paradox at play. The more I realize how small I am, the more I touch something that feels infinite.

The more I let go of my ego, the more I feel connected to everything.

Echoes of Advaita: One Reality, Many Forms

Advaita Vedanta, the ancient Indian philosophy, points to this very mystery. It says that the "I" I usually refer to - my name, my story, my body - is a limited expression of a single, undivided reality. According to this view, there are not two things - the universe and me - but only one.

But this is not a belief to be accepted. It is a question to be lived. What if the same awareness that allows me to experience the stars is not separate from the source of the stars themselves? What if the same consciousness that sees, hears, and feels is not *inside* me, but is *what I truly am*, beyond form? What if my sense of being a separate "I" is only a useful illusion - like a wave thinking it is separate from the ocean?

The Universe as a Mirror

I may never know all the scientific details of dark matter, black holes, or quantum fields. But I know this: when I sit silently and observe the universe, it reflects something back to me - not information, but insight.

The stars do not speak, but they whisper of stillness. The galaxies do not teach, but they show me how to let go. The cosmos does not ask questions, but in its silence, it invites me to return to the most essential question of all:

What is this "I" that sees the universe - and feels connected to it?

What This Means for My Life

When I believe I am the centre of the world, everything feels urgent - every failure is a disaster, every success is a validation. But when I remember my place in the cosmos, my perspective changes. I take myself less seriously - but not in a way that diminishes me. Rather, I feel more free. I no longer need to control everything. I no longer fear every setback. I no longer crave to be someone extraordinary.

Because I see now that just being alive, just being aware, just being here - is already extraordinary. The universe has no need for me to be special. And in realizing that, I find a strange liberation. I still live. I still love. I still work and dream and grow. But I do so without clinging so tightly to the illusion that everything depends on me.

And perhaps, in letting go of that illusion, I come closer - not to emptiness, but to wholeness.

Chapter 34

The Infinite "I" – The Final Realization

For much of my life, I searched for meaning - in work, in relationships, in success, in ambition, and in the pursuit of purpose itself. Each stage of this journey was shaped by who I believed I was. I built my identity through experiences, roles, achievements, and attachments. I sought stability in work, validation in relationships, fulfilment in accomplishments. But as time passed, I began to realize that everything I clung to was temporary.

I once believed that "I" was the sum of everything I had built - my career, my relationships, my successes, my failures. That my worth was tied to what I could prove, to what I could hold onto. But I have watched as everything I thought was "me" changed - my thoughts evolved, my desires shifted, my body aged, my ambitions transformed. If everything I identified with kept evolving, then who am I beyond all these changes?

This question has followed me through every stage of life. I spent years trying to create stability, to control outcomes, to build a life that would protect me from uncertainty. But the more I tried to hold onto things, the more I realized that I was grasping at illusions. The nature of life itself is impermanence. Nothing remains the same, no matter how tightly I hold on. The world around me changes, the people I love change, and even my own thoughts and desires change. If everything I once believed to be "me" is constantly shifting, then what is truly mine?

The Illusion of Separation

I resisted this realization for years, fearing that if I let go, there would be nothing left. But slowly, I began to see that letting go is not an ending - it is a return to something deeper. The ancient rishis of India saw this long before I did. They declared: *"Aham Brahmasmi"* - *I Am Brahman.*

At first, this phrase seemed abstract, almost mystical. What does it mean to say "I am Brahman"? Does it mean I am God? Does it mean I no longer exist as an individual? I struggled with this, trying to fit it into the framework of the identity I had built. But the truth of these words is not about individual greatness; it is about the dissolution of the illusion of separateness.

Aham Brahmasmi does not mean I become infinite - it means I was never separate from the infinite to begin with.

The Wave and the Ocean – The Truth of Non-Separation

For most of my life, I saw myself as an independent being, separate from the world, navigating life on my own terms. But I now see that this separation was only in my mind.

The wave believes it is separate from the ocean because it has its own form, its own movement, its own rise and fall. But when it crashes back into the sea, it realizes it was never separate - it was ocean all along. In the same way, I believed I was a distinct self, isolated in my body and mind. But in truth, the body, the mind, and the self I thought I was, were never apart from the vastness of existence.

I spent my life believing I was an individual traveller on a journey. But now I see - I was never a traveller; I was always the journey itself.

So What? What Does This Mean for Me?

For the lay reader, for the one who asks, "What does this realization mean for me? How does it change my life?" - the answer is simple, yet profound. It means that I no longer have to live in fear.

The fear of failure loses its power when I realize that failure only exists when I define myself by temporary achievements. If my essence is infinite, then no single success or failure can define me. The fear of loss dissolves when I understand that nothing was ever truly mine to lose. The people I love, the things I own, even my own body - none of it is separate from the larger whole. What I lose only changes form.

The fear of death weakens when I recognize that death is only the dissolution of the temporary. If I was never just this body, then what dies? The body returns to the earth, but what I truly am does not vanish. The fear of the unknown fades when I realize that the unknown is only frightening when I believe I am separate from it. But if I am part of all existence, what is there to fear?

This realization does not mean I stop engaging with life. It does not mean I abandon my responsibilities, my relationships, or my experiences. In fact, it allows me to live more fully than ever before.

If I am not defined by my job, I can work without the anxiety of success or failure. If I am not bound by attachments, I can love freely, without possessiveness or insecurity. If I am not controlled by fear, I can experience life with complete presence, without worrying about what comes next.

Living as the Infinite "I"

This is not a philosophy to be intellectually understood; it is a truth to be lived. It does not mean retreating from the world, renouncing all ambition, or withdrawing into detachment. It means engaging with life more deeply, but without the weight of illusion.

I can still chase my goals, but with the awareness that my worth is not tied to them. I can still build relationships, but without the fear of loss. I can still love, still dream, still create, knowing that whatever I experience is simply part of the flow of existence.

This realization brings freedom. A freedom not from life, but within it. *Aham Brahmasmi* does not change what I do - it changes how I experience everything.

The Final Letting Go – A Return, Not an End

For so long, I resisted letting go. I feared loss, I feared change, and most of all, I feared disappearing. I feared that if I let go of everything, nothing would remain. But now, as I stand at the threshold of the greatest transition - the dissolution of the self - I see that letting go is not the end; it is the return to what was always true. I am not losing myself - I am returning to myself. I am not vanishing into the unknown - I am merging with the infinite.

Letting go has always been the greatest challenge. Throughout my life, I have had to let go of many things - youth, certainty, loved ones, ambitions that no longer served me. And now, as I prepare for the final letting go, I understand that death is not an ending; it is a return. It is not a loss; it is a dissolution into something greater than I ever imagined. The waves crash upon the shore, but the ocean remains. The flame extinguishes, but the fire still exists. The body fades, but what I truly am does not disappear.

The Ultimate Realization

Aham Brahmasmi.

I was never just this temporary self. I was never just this passing experience. I have always been the infinite reality itself. And now, as I let go of the last illusion of separation, I do not disappear - I dissolve into everything. Because the "I" that I thought I was, was never real.

The reality that I truly am has no beginning and no end. And that is the greatest freedom of all.

This Page has been intentionally left Blank

The Journey Continues

There is no final truth - only deeper seeing

From the very beginning of this book, the question has never been, *What should I become?* but *Who have I always been, beneath all becoming?*

Each chapter has offered a mirror - sometimes showing the face of identity, sometimes the shadow of fear, sometimes the vast sky of possibility. We have walked through memory, conditioning, success, failure, ambition, desire, purpose, love, loss, and death - not as topics to be mastered, but as windows through which to glimpse the elusive presence we call *"I."*

And now we reach the final page. But if you have truly followed the thread of this book, you may already feel that this is not a conclusion – it is a widening. A soft expansion into the awareness that *the journey of self is not linear, and it is never complete.*

What Has Changed?

Not the world. Not the roles. Not the facts of life. But perhaps something in your seeing.

Perhaps you now notice the quiet observer behind your emotions. Perhaps you are able to sit with uncertainty without needing to label it. Perhaps you have begun to sense that *the "I" you believed yourself to be was a story - one that can now be gently rewritten, or released.* If so, this book has served its purpose.

There Are No Answers Here

You may have come looking for conclusions. But what this book hopes to offer is not closure, but space. Not knowledge, but clarity. Not dogma, but freedom.

The truth of *I* - the Infinite Reality - is not something that can be captured in a sentence or even a single book. It is not a philosophy to be believed, but a presence to be sensed. It is not reached through logic alone, but through inquiry, reflection, and awareness. The Infinite "I" is not an idea. It is the very awareness through which all ideas arise.

The Journey Ahead Is Yours

There is no final teaching to give. No wisdom to transfer. No secret to whisper. There is only a gentle invitation - to watch, to feel, to inquire, to unlearn, to rest.

As life continues to unfold, this book may fade from memory. But *if the questioning has taken root*, the journey will continue. It will move quietly, under the surface of every thought, every encounter, every silence. Not always as clarity, but often as wonder.

You will forget, and you will remember. That is the nature of the path. And through it all, something unchanging will remain - **You.** Or rather - *the infinite you.* The one who has always been watching. The one who has no name, no form, and no end.

233

This Page has been intentionally left Blank

About the Author

Jayan Menon is a senior leader in the banking and technology sectors and an All-India rank holder Chartered Accountant. Over the course of his career, he has held leadership roles at large institutions including TATA Steel, ICICI Bank, YES Bank, and Tata Consultancy Services, and served as CEO of the Fixed Income Money Market and Derivatives Association of India (FIMMDA).

He has contributed to several high-level financial committees, including those of FIMMDA, the Foreign Exchange Dealers' Association of India (FEDAI), the Indian Banks' Association (IBA), and SWIFT (Society for Worldwide Interbank Financial Telecommunication), headquartered in Belgium.

Jayan has been invited to speak at prestigious institutions such as the National Institute of Bank Management (NIBM) and the Bankers' Training College and has addressed students at leading management institutes. He also served as the guiding voice behind *The Practitioner's Guide to Trade Finance* (Taxmann).

Beyond his professional career, Jayan is a long-time student of philosophy, deeply influenced by Advaita Vedanta, Buddhism, and Stoicism. Equally passionate about emerging technology, he closely follows developments in artificial intelligence, digital platforms, and technology regulation, and holds a Diploma in Cyber Law from the Asian School of Cyber Laws.

His interest in the intersection of technology and human potential led him to found *sainterview* - a company focused on autonomous, intelligent interview platforms.

Not the end,
only the unfolding of what truly is.

www.ingramcontent.com/pod-product-compliance
Lightning Source LLC
Chambersburg PA
CBHW060530160726
47991CB00001B/265